Japanese for All Occasions

CHARLES E. TUTTLE COMPANY
Tokyo, Japan & Rutland, Vermont

Japanese
for All
Occasions

The Right Word at the Right Time

Anne Kaneko

Illustrations by
Sally Motomura

Published by the Charles E. Tuttle Company, Inc.
of Rutland, Vermont & Tokyo, Japan
with editorial offices at
2–6 Suido 1-chome, Bunkyo-ku, Tokyo 112

© 1990 by Charles E. Tuttle, Co., Inc.

Library of Congress Catalog Card No. 89-51719
International Standard Book No. 0-8048-1567-4

First edition, 1991
Fourth printing, 1994

Printed in Japan

Acknowledgments

Since I am a non-native speaker, I have had to rely on the assistance of many Japanese people. I am grateful to Mrs. Kazuko Shimizu for painstakingly checking the manuscript; to Mr. Koichi Mitani; to Mr. Hiroshi Ishino of the NHK Broadcasting Culture Research Institute for his information on respect language; and to Mrs. Mitsuko Kinoshita for doing the calligraphy in the final chapter on letters. I would also like to thank my non-Japanese friends. In particular, I owe much to Mr. Stephen Gomersall, formerly of the British Embassy in Tokyo, an accomplished speaker who contributed the introduction to the chapter on speeches and gave invaluable advice concerning wedding speeches; Drs. Michael and Lesley Connors, without whose support the manuscript would never have been completed; and Mrs. Sally Motomura for her sensitive illustrations.

To Naochika

Contents

Introduction

Japanese for All Occasions will help you speak useful, practical Japanese. With this handbook, you can quickly look up what to say for over two hundred situations covering all facets of everyday life. Whether you need to talk to an airport immigration official or to your next-door neighbor, you will be able to speak smoothly and correctly with the help of this book.

You will find that this is both a good book to browse through as well as a handy reference book to consult as the need arises. Let us first look at how the contents are presented.

The book begins with a chapter on basic expressions, an introduction to the many different ways of greeting, thanking, and apologizing in Japanese. Starting with chapter two, the book presents fourteen chapters, each dealing with one general topic. In other words, one chapter is devoted to shopping, another to traveling, another to business, and so on.

Each chapter is then subdivided into sections covering specific situations. For instance, included in the chapter on traveling are sections showing what to say when you rent a car, buy a train ticket, reserve a hotel room, and so forth. These sections include both example sentences and situational dialogues based on actual conversations. Concluding each chapter after chapter one is a glossary of useful words and expressions.

As this book is not a programmed course in Japanese, you can skip directly to any chapter you want. In other words, when you are confronted with a certain situation, go straight to the relevant chapter. For example, if you have been asked to speak at a Japanese wedding, refer to chapter eleven for guidance on what to do and what to say. Or if your washing machine breaks down, consult chapter four for help in explaining the problem over the telephone to the repairman.

Although *Japanese for All Occasions* is written especially for those with a basic command of Japanese, beginners will discover that, with the help of this book, they too will quickly gain confidence in interacting smoothly with the Japanese. Even a beginner who learns only the basic expressions presented in chapter one will witness a dramatic improvement in his or her ability to deal with many ordinary situations.

A word of advice for any student of Japanese: learn to recognize the importance of nonverbal communication. Because hesitancy is interpreted in Japan as a sign of good social manners, not as an indication of inadequate knowledge, foreigners need not worry about speaking slowly and deliberately. As will be explained further in chapter one, when you must refuse something, polite hemming and hawing often can prevent bad will.

Another simple piece of advice is this: rather than dwelling on what the actual meanings of difficult Japanese words and expressions are, concentrate instead on learning *when* to use them. Mastering the usage of set Japanese expressions immensely improves the way you sound to native speakers.

A few points explaining the premises on which this book has been based should be mentioned here. The first point deals with colloquial language. As you go through the dialogues, you may notice that the Japanese sometimes differs from what you have studied in ordinary textbooks. More so in Japanese than in English, the spoken word varies from the written word, and what may be standard practice in speech might not be acceptable in writing. Because this book focuses on colloquial Japanese, grammar rules sometimes have been broken so as to give the reader an accurate picture of what actually is said. For example, the particles *o* and *wa* have been omitted, respectively, before *o-negai shimasu* and *irasshaimasu ka* in many of the dialogues. These two omissions have been marked by commas, since most speakers pause at this point in the sentence.

Another point is that the abbreviation of *no* to just *n* in colloquial speech has been indicated in this book by adding an apostrophe after the *n* and joining it to the previous word. For instance, *iku no desu* in its abbreviated form appears as *ikun' desu*.

Unless specifically stated in the explanations, the expressions and dialogues are suitable for either men or women; in most of the dialogues, male and female roles of the speakers have been chosen arbitrarily. Also, because ordinary conversation tends to cover much small talk that would be impossible to include in this book, many of the dialogues have been condensed. Elapses of time within a dialogue have been indicated by three consecutive asterisks.

Generally speaking, the translations of the Japanese express what one would say in English under similar conditions. However, equivalent, word-for-word translations are not always possible. Where the English translation strays too far from the Japanese or where a Japanese expression cannot be translated into natural English, literal translations often have been included in parentheses. For example, the English translation for *Itsumo o-sewa ni narimasu,* a common everyday expression in Japanese but one with no good English equivalent, is frequently given in parentheses as "I'm always indebted to you."

Finally, keep in mind that Japanese customs and language differ depending on locality, social environment, and individual preference. This book will help you understand what often happens and what often is said; if in actuality you find discrepancies, adjust accordingly to what people around you do and say.

1 The Fundamentals

GREETINGS AND OTHER set expressions help any society run smoothly. In Japan, these phrases delineate relationships, offer face-saving ways to deal with difficult situations, and provide a convenient shorthand to express thanks or regret. It is well worth your time to learn the expressions in this chapter; in many situations, there is no phrase better than the set phrase.

Greeting People

Following are some of the most common expressions used for greeting people.

Ohayō gozaimasu. Good morning.
  Literally meaning "It is early," *Ohayō gozaimasu* was originally an expression of gratitude said to workers who arrived early. Friends often drop the *gozaimasu* when greeting each other.

Konnichi wa. Good afternoon./Hello.
  Used from around midday to late afternoon, this greeting has a much more limited application than "Hello" or *Ohayō gozaimasu*. *Konnichi wa* is usually not said to colleagues or family members, and with the exception perhaps of neighbors, it is seldom used to address someone of higher rank.

Konban wa. Good evening.
  Like *Konnichi wa*, this greeting is somewhat more limited in its use than *Ohayō gozaimasu*. If you are living with a Japanese family, your use of either *Konnichi wa* or *Konban wa* may sound standoffish; in other words, it may give the wrong impression that you do not want to be treated like the other members of the family.

Shitsurei shimasu./O-jama shimasu. Excuse me. (*lit.*, I will disturb you.)
  Either one of these two polite expressions would be an appropriate remark when entering or leaving another person's home or office.

osaki ni shitsurei shimasu (when leaving before others)

shitsurei desuga ..... (Excuse me but .....)

18

Tadaima. I'm home!

This expression is said when one has just returned home. The response by those in the house is *Okaeri-nasai* (Welcome home). Said by a waiter in a restaurant, *tadaima* means "right away."

Follow-up Expressions

Japanese frequently follow up a greeting with one of the phrases listed here.

Konaida wa dōmo./Senjitsu wa dōmo. Thank you for the other day.

These two phrases express gratitude for something that was recently done. They are also often used simply as opening remarks when people meet or telephone each other. If you wish to be more polite, say *Konaida/Senjitsu wa dōmo arigatō gozaimashita* (Thank you for the other day) or *Konaida/Senjitsu wa dōmo gochisō-sama deshita* (Thank you for the meal/drinks the other day).

O-hisashiburi desu ne./Shibaraku-buri desu ne. It's been a long time.

A common response to either of these two phrases is *Go-busata shite imasu* (Sorry not to have been in touch).

Keiki wa dō desu ka? How's business?/How's everything with you?

This expression is frequently used in business situations. Variations include the more informal *Keiki wa dō?* and the more polite *Keiki wa ikaga desu ka?* A good response is *Hai, o-kagesama desu,* which means "Fine, thank you" (*lit.*, thanks to you).

Osaka businessmen greet each other with *Mōkarimakka?* (*lit.*, Making money?) The standard reply is *Bochi-bochi* or *Botsu-botsu desu wa,* both literally meaning "a bit at a time."

O-isogashii desu ka? Are you busy?/Have you been busy?

One response to this might be *Mā-mā desu ne* (Not bad).

Dōmo./Dōmo dōmo. Thanks.

Dōmo is an all-encompassing expression of thanks and apology that is widely used, especially by men. This word can be used with

Domo sumimasen.

almost any of the other set expressions in this chapter, e.g., *Dōmo, konnichi wa* (Hello) and *Dōmo, o-hisashiburi* (It's been a while).

Commenting on the Weather

Upon meeting someone, if you don't have anything in particular to say, you can always say something about the weather. Here is a selection that should get you through most types of weather.

- *Samui desu ne.*
  It's cold, isn't it?
- *Ame ga futte kimashita ne.*
  It's started to rain, hasn't it?
- *Haremashita ne.*
  It's cleared up, hasn't it?
- *Uttōshii tenki desu ne.*   *Uttōshii Kimochini narimasu*
  It's dreary weather, isn't it?
- *Atatakaku narimashita ne.*
  It's really warming up, isn't it?
- *Ii o-tenki desu ne.*
  It's beautiful weather, isn't it?
- *Atsukute, taihen desu ne.*
  It's awfully hot, isn't it?
- *Mushi-atsui desu ne.*
  It's hot and humid, isn't it?

Being Introduced

When meeting someone for the first time, most people in Japan use the following set expression:

- *Hajimemashite. Dōzo yoroshiku o-negai shimasu.*
  How do you do? Pleased to meet you.

This expression points out that it is a first-time meeting and then asks for the other person's favorable consideration. The standard reply is:

- *Kochira koso. Dōzo yoroshiku.*
  The pleasure's mine. Glad to meet you.

Saying Goodbye

Following are some of the most common expressions used when parting from people.

Sayōnara. Goodbye. (*lit.,* If it must be so.)

Unfortunately, this famous and romantic farewell is not used so much. Although schoolchildren are taught to say *Sayōnara* to their teachers at the end of the school day, adults do not usually use it in ordinary situations. *Sayōnara* is mostly used between friends when they are parting for a long time; for example, when they are seeing off someone who is moving to a different place.

Shitsurei shimasu. Goodbye. (*lit.,* Excuse me for what I am going to do.)

This polite phrase is used in business situations, at social gatherings, or when leaving someone's home.

Dewa mata. See you./Bye!

Dewa mata is a common way for friends to say goodbye. You may also hear variations like *Mata raishū* (See you next week); *Mata ashita* (See you tomorrow); and *Ja mata* and *Izure mata* (See you).

Baibai. Bye-bye.

Young people, especially children, use this expression. Also commonly used by young people are *Jā* and *Jā ne*.

Gochisō-sama deshita. Thank you./It was delicious.

This expression is always said as soon as you have finished eating or drinking something. It is often repeated when bidding goodbye to someone who has treated you to a meal (or even to just a cup of tea), and it can also be said by customers to the staff of a restaurant upon leaving the premises.

Oyasumi-nasai. Good night.

Frequently used on the telephone, this expression is a common

21

way for friends and family to say good night. *Oyasumi-nasai* generally is not used, however, when you leave the company at the end of a working day; it would imply that those remaining at the office would sleep there until morning! Use *O-saki ni* instead.

O-saki ni. Goodbye./Excuse me, but I have to leave. (*lit.,* Excuse me for going ahead of you.)

This expression, whose more polite form is *O-saki ni shitsurei shimasu,* is used when leaving a group of friends or fellow workers. The appropriate response in work situations would be *Go-kurōsama deshita* or *O-tsukaresama deshita.* (Goodbye./Thank you for your help.)

Itte kimasu. Goodbye./I'm off! (*lit.,* I'll go and come back.)

This phrase, whose more polite form is *Itte mairimasu,* is used when leaving home. It is also used during working hours when people temporarily leave their offices. The appropriate response by those remaining is *Itte'rasshai* (*lit.,* Go).

O-daiji ni. Take care of your health.

This friendly phrase is used when taking leave of the elderly or of someone who is sick or injured.

Okyotsukene Take care of yourself.

Go-kigen yō. Farewell.

This expression can sound either refined or affected depending on the circumstances. Although you may seldom hear friends say this, *Go-kigen yō* frequently is used as a farewell greeting on television and radio shows.

Ja, ki o tsukete. Take care.

This casual farewell phrase is used between friends. More polite, but still friendly, equivalents are *O-ki o tsukete* and *Dōzo, o-genki de*.

Expressing Gratitude

Although there are many ways to express gratitude in Japanese, the following expressions are perhaps the ones most commonly used.

Arigatō. Thank you.

This expression has several forms. From informal to very polite, they are: *Dōmo arigatō, Arigatō gozaimasu*, and *Dōmo arigatō gozaimasu*.

While it is difficult to give clear-cut rules, here are some guidelines for using the past tense and the present tense of this expression. When the action is happening or will happen, say *Arigatō gozaimasu*: e.g., when you are being handed a present. When the action is completed, say *Arigatō gozaimashita*: e.g., when you have received a present in the mail and are thanking the sender by telephone. An appropriate response to *Arigatō* is *Dō itashimashite* (You're welcome).

Sumimasen. Thank you.

This expression is often used to thank someone who has done or will do something for you. Similar expressions for thanking someone who has finished doing something for you are *Go-meiwaku o kakemashita* and *O-tesū o kakemashita*. As with *Arigatō*, a good response to *Sumimasen* is *Dō itashimashite* (You're welcome). Note that *Sumimasen* is also used as an apology (*see* page 27).

O-sewa ni narimashita. Thank you for your help. (*lit.,* I'm obliged to you.)

This phrase is the best way to express gratitude to someone who has spent some of his or her time helping you. When you want to thank someone who has shown you around, say something like:

• *Taihen o-sewa ni narimashita. Iro-iro go-annai itadaite, tottemo yokatta desu.*

Thank you very much for all your kindness. It was wonderful to have you take us around.

In its present tense, *Itsumo o-sewa ni narimasu* is used as a set expression to greet a person who regularly does something for you. For instance, parents say this to their child's teachers at school functions, and businessmen say this to their clients. It is used very often on the telephone.

Tasukarimashita. You've been a great help.

This expression is often used in conjunction with *Okage-sama de* (Thanks to you). If someone has helped you with a translation, you can thank them like this:

• *Okage-sama de shime-kiri ni ma-ni-atte, hontō ni tasukarimashita.*

Thanks to you I made the deadline. You were a great help.

Gokurō-sama. Goodbye./Thank you for your help.

This is a traditional phrase expressing appreciation to someone who has finished working. For instance, people say this to fellow workers who have ended their day's work and are on their way home. In fact, you can use this expression to thank just about anyone who has done a job or service for you; e.g., a delivery man, a repairman, or a house painter.

Many people feel this phrase is inappropriate when addressing superiors. You might be better off using *otsukare-sama* instead.

Otsukare-sama. Thank you for your help/work.

This phrase originated in the entertainment world and has spread by television into general usage. It is now interchangeable with *Gokurō-sama*, and perhaps even more widely used.

Kyōshuku desu. I am very grateful.

The literal meaning of this phrase is "I shrink with fear (in the face of your great kindness)." If someone has unexpectedly done something nice to you, you can offer thanks by saying:

• *Sorewa-sorewa, dōmo, kyōshuku desu.*

This really is too much. Thank you.

Itadakimasu. Thank you./It looks delicious. (*lit.,* I receive.)

This expression is said before taking the first bite or drink of a meal or snack. Everyone says *Itadakimasu,* even the host. *Itadakimasu* is also used extensively as the polite form of the verb *morau* (receive).

Gochisō-sama deshita. Thank you (for the meal, snack, etc.).

This phrase is said after finishing a meal or snack. It is also used to say goodbye. (*see* page 21)

How to Avoid Saying "You"

Anata translates as "you," but its use is generally avoided. One exception is when wives call their husbands *anata*; then it has the special meaning of "darling."

When talking to someone, you can be safe and say his or her name, with the suffix *-san,* every time you want to say "you." Otherwise, refer to teachers, doctors, speakers, and government officials as *sensei,* and higher ranking members in your company by their titles. For example, if you want to ask your division manager what he plans to do, say *Buchō wa dō nasaimasu ka?*

How do you address the wife of a friend or the married woman next door? You can use either her last name, or if you need to make the distinction between her and her husband, you can call her *okusan.*

Quick Responses

Following is a sample of common expressions along with their appropriate responses. Note that although only one response is given for each expression, there may be other acceptable ways to respond.

EXPRESSION: *O-hisashiburi desu ne.* It's been a long time.

RESPONSE: *Go-busata shite imasu.* Sorry not to have been in touch.

EXPRESSION: *Dōmo arigatō.* Thank you.

RESPONSE: *Dō itashimashite.* You're welcome.

EXPRESSION: *Sumimasen.* I'm sorry.

RESPONSE: *Dō itashimashite.* That's all right.

EXPRESSION: *Tadaima.* I'm home.

RESPONSE: *Okaeri-nasai.* Welcome home.

EXPRESSION: *Itte kimasu.* I'm off!

RESPONSE: *Itte'rasshai.* Goodbye.

The Right Word

There is no need to be original or profuse in Japanese; often a well-timed phrase is all that is necessary. The following examples serve as a guide to what to say and how to respond in certain situations. Note that in the second example, most people would not bother to respond.

1. Accidentally bumping into someone on the subway
   A, shitsurei. Sorry.
   Iie. That's all right.
2. Pushing your way to the door on a crowded bus
   Sumimasen. Excuse me.
3. Apologizing to a next-door neighbor after causing a loud disturbance
   Urusakute, sumimasen. I'm sorry about the loud racket.
   Otagai-sama desukara. That's all right (*lit.,* It's give and take.)
4. Thanking someone who has given you a present
   Arigatō gozaimasu. Thank you very much.
   Dō itashimashite. Not at all.
5. Thanking someone who has given you directions
   Dōmo sumimasen deshita. Sorry to have troubled you.
   Iie. Not at all.

6. Letting someone go before you
  Dōzo./O-saki ni dōzo. After you.
  Arigatō. Thank you.
7. Introducing yourself to someone
  Hajimemashite. Dōzo yoroshiku. Pleased to meet you.
  Kochira koso. Yoroshiku o-negai shimasu. The pleasure is mine.
8. Leaving the office
  O-saki ni shitsurei shimasu. Goodbye.
  Gokurō-sama deshita. Goodbye.
9. Getting service at a store counter
  Sumimasen! Excuse me!
  Hai. Sugu mairimasu. I'll be right there.
10. Calling at the door of someone's home
  Gomen kudasai! Hello? Is anyone there?
  Hai! Coming!
11. Getting ready to take a first bite
  Itadakimasu. Looks delicious.
  Dōzo. Please go ahead.
12. Thanking someone for a meal, snack, etc.
  Gochisō-sama deshita. Thank you. It was delicious.
  Dō itashimashite. You're welcome.

Apologizing

A Japanese's first reaction to many situations is to apologize. All apologies should be accompanied by bows.

Sumimasen. I am sorry.

Besides being the most widely used apology, *Sumimasen* is also used to attract attention and to express thanks. Polite forms include *Dōmo sumimasen deshita* and *Aisumimasen.*

Shitsurei shimashita. I am sorry.

This expression is another commonly used apology. For the many people who confuse it with its present-tense form, *Shitsurei shimasu,* it might help to think of *Shitsurei shimasu* as "Excuse me

27

CHAPTER 1

for what I'm going to do" and *Shitsurei shimashita* as "Excuse me for what I've done."

Shitsurei shimashita, being more polite than *Sumimasen,* is recommended for business situations. If you accidentally interrupt your boss when he has a visitor, you can say:

• *A, shitsurei shimashita. Mata mairimasu.*
  Oh, I'm sorry. I'll come back later.

Mōshi-wake arimasen. I am very sorry. (*lit.,* There is no excuse.)
  This expression is more polite than *Sumimasen* or *Shitsurei shimashita.* Its polite form is *Mōshi-wake gozaimasen.*

omatase shite sumimasen deshita — past tense

O-matase shimashita. Sorry to have kept you waiting.
  This phrase is a courteous way to apologize to someone who has been kept waiting. It is used frequently on the telephone.

Gomen-nasai. Sorry.
  Repentant children bow their heads and say *Gomen-nasai* when they have done wrong. Since by itself *gomen-nasai* can sound too familiar, you might want to follow it with more apologies like in the following example:

• *A, gomen-nasai. Sumimasen deshita. Daijōbu desu ka?*
  Oh, pardon. I'm sorry. Are you all right?

Asking Permission

A simple way to ask permission is to use the present tense *-te* (or *-de*) form of a verb and attach *ii desu ka?* Adding *mo* after the verb adds emphasis to the request.

• *Naka ni haitte (mo) ii desu ka?*
  May I come in?

If a situation requires tact, you might want to use the causative *-te* (or *-de*) form of the verb, and replace *ii desu ka?* with *kudasaimasen ka?*

• *Ashita yasumasete kudasaimasen ka?*
  Could I please have tomorrow off?

Ashita oyasumio itadakemasen deshō ka?

28

When you need to choose your words very carefully, replace *kudasaimasen ka?* with *itadakitain' desu ga.*
 • *Ashita yasumasete itadakitain' desu ga...*
 Could you possibly let me have tomorrow off?

This complicated construction is humble because of the causative *yasumasete,* polite because of the humble *itadakitai,* and softened because of the *desu ga...* No one will be able to withhold his permission in the face of such politeness!

Making Requests

Following are several different ways to ask someone to do something.

O-negai shimasu. Please. (*lit.,* I request.)
 This expression is used when making requests. The object particle *o* is frequently dropped before *o-negai shimasu* in colloquial speech (but seldom in writing). When asking for someone on the phone, say:
 • *Yamada-san, o-negai shimasu.*
 Mr. Yamada, please./I would like to speak with Mr. Yamada.

Kudasai. Please.
 Generally speaking, *kudasai* is used in two ways. When it follows a noun, *kudasai* means "give (me)."
 • *A-ranchi kudasai.*
 May I please have the "A" lunch?

When used after the *-te* form of a verb, *kudasai* means "Could you please."
 • *Ashita kite kudasai.*
 Could you please come tomorrow.

If you wish to be more polite, replace *kudasai* with *kudasaimasen ka?*
 • *Nihon-go o oshiete kudasaimasen ka?*
 Would you please teach me Japanese?

29

Moraemasu ka?/Itadakemasu ka? (*lit.,* May I receive?)

Two verbs meaning to receive, *morau* and the politer *itadaku*, are widely used when making requests. Negative forms of these verbs make the request more polite.

- *Chotto matte moraemasu ka?/itadakemasu ka?*
  Would you mind waiting a moment?
- *Sumimasen. Kore o dokete moraemasen ka?/itadakemasen ka?*
  Excuse me. Would you mind moving this?

Leading up to a Request

Rather than abruptly making a request, you might prepare the listener for what is to follow by starting with one of these phrases.

- *Ashita no kaigi no koto nan' desu ga . . .*
  About tomorrow's meeting . . .
- *Jitsu wa, o-negai ga atte, o-denwa shita/wake nan' desu ga . . .*
  I phoned because there was something I wanted to ask you . . .
- *O-isogashii tokoro, sumimasen.*
  I'm sorry to disturb you when you're busy.

Refusing Requests

Although refusals should be made discreetly, it is important to make it clear whether you are refusing or accepting. At the first hint of something undesirable, you might want to make a remark such as:

- *Sō desu ne . . .*
  Well . . .

When the request comes, it is often enough to say:

- *Sā, chotto . . .*
  Well, it's just that . . .

When spoken hesitantly, with pauses before and after the *chotto*, either phrase below should convey your desire not to partake.

- *Konogoro, chotto, shigoto ga isogashikute.*
  I'm rather busy at work these days.

• *Saikin, chotto, taichō o kuzushimashite.*
I've really not been feeling well recently.

If you cannot think of a specific reason, you could play for time.
• *Chotto sōdan shite, mata o-denwa shimasu.*
I'll discuss it (with someone) and call you back.
• *Chotto kangaesasete kudasai. Daiji na koto desukara.*
Please let me think it over. It's such an important matter.

Obviously, specific excuses make convincing refusals:
• *Sumimasen ga, kyūyō ga dekimashita node.*
I'm sorry, but something urgent has come up.
• *Zannen desu ga, hatsuka wa tsugō ga warui no desu ga.*
I'm afraid I'm not free on the twentieth.
• *Hidoi kaze o hiite shimaimashita. Utsuru to ikenai desukara.*
I've got a terrible cold. I wouldn't like you to get it.

In cases when your reasons still do not convince the listener,
you can try one of these statements:
• *Mōshi-wake arimasen ga, konkai wa o-yaku ni tatemasen node.*
I'm sorry but I can't help you this time.
• *Zannen desu ga, kondo wa enryo sasete itadakimasu.*
I'm sorry but I ~~can't help~~ m going to have to decline this time.
• *Demo komarimasu.*
But that would put me in a bind.

On the other side of the coin, you may fall victim to a reluctance
of the Japanese to give a direct refusal. Japanese have a tendency
to stress the positive "I really would like to go" and not the negative
"But I can't." Certain Japanese phrases that sound positive in
fact are often refusals. A good example is this phrase:
• *Mae-muki ni kentō sasete moraimasu.*
We will consider it constructively.

The oblique phrase and delaying tone are enough to tell any
Japanese that the situation is difficult. One must learn to read
between the lines.

2 The Neighborhood

TRADITIONALLY, one's neighbors were the three houses across the street and the houses on each side, *mukō san-gen, ryō-donari*; more often than not, this close-knit unit operated like one big family. Even today in some districts, neighbors exchange food, help at funerals, and share extravagant gifts. Presenting a neighbor with a few homemade cookies or sharing something with them from your country will be interpreted as a gesture of friendship. You will certainly receive something in return.

You might find that your Japanese neighbors are more tolerant than you are. The prevailing attitude is one of give-and-take, *otagai-sama*. You put up with their noisy dog and they tolerate your noisy children; your guests can park in front of their gate if their guests can park in front of yours. If you will be the source of disturbance, you can smooth relations with a prior warning, or failing that, an explanation afterward. Small gifts from time to time can help maintain good relationships with the neighbors.

Living in a Japanese community requires certain responsibilities. For example, various dues may have to be paid to the town association. Trash is to be put out only on certain days, and in some areas, people take turns cleaning the collection point after the garbage truck has left. Neighbors may not look kindly on those who do not abide by these communal rules.

If you wish to take an active part in your community, the *chōnai-kai* (town association) will be only too happy to have your help. These bodies, linked both with the city or ward office and with the police and fire departments, are responsible primarily for disseminating information on health, sanitation, and the environment. They also organize outings, local festivals, and other community activities. You can join the Sunday morning weeding group or the pest-control squad, help supervise baseball practice for children, or participate in planning (and celebrating) the local festival.

If you are new to the area, ask your neighbors about nearby stores, schools, doctors, and so forth. The local policeman too will gladly recommend good places, as will the postman and the Yakult lady, the woman who delivers sweet, yogurt-type drinks by bicycle. These people know the entire area and therefore are mines of information. Also, do not be afraid to try local markets and family-run shops; you will find the service far more friendly than at the large grocery stores.

Unfortunately, some of your encounters with people in your neighborhood may not be so pleasant. In particular, you may find it very bothersome to cope with the door-to-door salespeople selling everything from contraceptives and fire extinguishers to money-making and money-saving plans.

This chapter will help you deal successfully with the people in your community, whether they be pushy salesmen or friendly neighbors. Even if you have limited language skills, you will be surprised how much a little Japanese will help make your home life in Japan more enjoyable.

Calling on the Neighbors

Your neighbors will probably be the group of five to ten houses around which notices are circulated; if you live in an apartment, they might be the tenants on your floor and perhaps those who share the same staircase.

In Japan, a new arrival visits the neighbors, often distributing a small gift.

NEW ARRIVAL:

Gomen kudasai. Kondo, ue no kai no sanbyaku-ni gō-shitsu ni hikkoshite kimashita Kūpā desu. Dōzo yoroshiku.

Hello. My name is Cooper and I've just moved into apartment 302 on the next floor. Pleased to meet you.

WOMAN:

Kochira koso. Nihon wa nagain' desu ka?

The pleasure's mine. Have you been in Japan long?

NEW ARRIVAL:

Sangatsu kara desu.

Since March.

WOMAN:

Sō desu ka? Moshi wakaranai koto ga attara, osshatte kudasai ne.

Oh, really? If there's anything you want to know, please ask.

NEW ARRIVAL:

Arigatō gozaimasu. Dewa, sassoku desu ga, gomi wa itsu daseba ii desu ka?

Thank you. Well, for starters I was wondering when to put the trash out.

WOMAN:

Nama-gomi wa Ges-Sui-Kin, moenai gomi wa Kayōbi desu. Asa hachi-ji made ni kanrinin-shitsu no ura ni daseba ii desu.

Kitchen refuse and paper is picked up on Mondays, Wednesdays, and Fridays. Garbage that can't be burned is picked up on Tuesdays. You have to take it behind the caretaker's apartment by 8:00 a.m.

NEW ARRIVAL:

Hai, wakarimashita. Arigatō gozaimasu. Dewa yoroshiku o-negai shimasu.

I see. Thank you. I look forward to seeing you again.

Asking About Restaurants

In this dialogue, a man asks a neighbor to recommend a restaurant that he can telephone to have food delivered to his home.

NEW ARRIVAL:

Konnichi wa.

Hello.

NEIGHBOR:

Konnichi wa.

Hello.

NEW ARRIVAL:

Mai-nichi atsui desu ne.

It's been so hot every day, hasn't it?

NEIGHBOR:

Hontō ne.

It certainly has been.

NEW ARRIVAL:

Tokoro de, konaida demae o tanomō to omottan' desu ga, oishii tokoro ga wakaranakute. Doko-ka ii tokoro, arimasen ka?

By the way, the other day I wanted to have some food delivered but I didn't know which restaurant would be good. Can you recommend one?

NEIGHBOR:

Doko ga iin' deshō ne. Kinjo no sushi-ya ga todokete kureru kedo amari oishikunain' desu yo. Tonkatsu-ya ga ii deshō. Nandemo arimasu kara. Chotto matte. Denwa bangō o shirabete kimasu kara. ∗ ∗ ∗ *Hai, dōzo.*

I wonder where would be best. The local sushi shop delivers but their sushi is not very good . . . You want the pork cutlet restaurant. It has everything. Just a minute and I'll get the telephone number. ∗ ∗ ∗ Here you are.

NEW ARRIVAL:

Arigatō gozaimasu. Tasukarimashita.

Thank you very much. That's a great help.

Ordering a Restaurant Delivery

By telephone, you can order a meal to be delivered to your door. The delivery may take twenty minutes or so but it will save you from having to cook and clean up. After you have finished eating, rinse the empty dishes and leave them outside your door. They will be picked up later.

CUSTOMER:

Demae, o-negai dekimasu ka?

Do you deliver?

RESTAURANT EMPLOYEE:

Hai, dōzo.

Yes, go ahead.

CUSTOMER:

Shōyu rāmen, mittsu o-negai shimasu.

Three bowls of soy-sauce noodles, please.

RESTAURANT EMPLOYEE:

Hai. Dochira-sama desu ka?

OK. May I have your name, please.

jusho = address

CUSTOMER:

Pāku Manshon no sanbyaku-ni gōshitsu no Kūpā desu.

Cooper. Apartment 302, Park Mansion.

RESTAURANT EMPLOYEE:

Hai. Tadaima.

Fine. We'll be right over.

CUSTOMER:

Narubeku hayaku o-negai shimasu.

Can you make it as soon as possible?

RESTAURANT EMPLOYEE:

Wakarimashita.

Certainly.

Admiring a Neighbor's Garden

Small, potted azaleas are a mass of flowers in May and June, and most enthusiasts will be delighted to show you their collections.

RESIDENT:

Ii tenki desu ne. Niwa-shigoto desu ka?

Beautiful day, isn't it? I see you're doing some gardening.

NEIGHBOR:

Ē, chotto.

Yes, a few odd jobs.

RESIDENT:

Shikashi, migoto na tsutsuji desu ne! Chotto mite ii desu ka?

Those really are splendid azaleas! May I take a look?

NEIGHBOR:
Dōzo, dōzo. Naka ni haitte mite kudasai.
Please do. Come inside and have a look.

RESIDENT:
Kore wa nensū ga tatte iru deshō.
This one must be very old.

NEIGHBOR:
Hyaku-nijū-nen mae no mono desu yo.
It's 120 years old.

RESIDENT:
Kanroku ga arimasu ne. Tenji-kai ni dasun' desu ka?
It's very impressive. Will you enter them in an exhibition?

NEIGHBOR:
Ē. Ima sono junbi ni kakatte imasu.
Yes. I'm getting them ready for one right now.

RESIDENT:
Subarashii desu. Arigatō gozaimashita.
Great. Thank you very much.

NEIGHBOR:
Iie. Mata dōzo.
Not at all. Come again.

Refusing Door-to-Door Salesmen

Pushy salesmen will enter your home and start displaying their wares in the hallway. If you are not interested in buying anything, it is best to make that clear right from the outset. The following dialogues cover three situations you may encounter.

PICKLE SALESMAN:
Kyōto no oishii tsuke-mono o motte kimashita ga, shishoku shite kudasai.
I have some delicious pickles from Kyoto. Would you like to try some?

RESIDENT:
Kekkō desu. Ma-ni-atte imasu.
No, thank you. We have enough.

* * *

knowledgable person

ENCYCLOPEDIA SALESMAN:

Hyakka-jiten wa ikaga desu ka? O-kosama no gakushū ni taihen benri desu yo.

Can I interest you in an encyclopedia? They're very useful for your child's schoolwork.

RESIDENT:

Sumimasen. Nihongo ga yomemasen node, kekkō desu.

I'm afraid we don't read Japanese. I'm sorry.

* * *

INVESTMENT-PLAN SALESWOMAN:

ABC Shōken desu ga, chochiku no go-annai ni ukagaimashita.

I'm from ABC Securities and I've come to tell you about our savings plans.

RESIDENT:

Shujin wa hoka no shōken-gaisha ni tsutomete imasu node, ABC-san wa chotto . . .

My husband works for another securities firm so I can't really do any business with ABC.

INVESTMENT-PLAN SALESWOMAN:

Sō desu ka. Shitsurei shimashita.

I see. Sorry to have disturbed you.

Disposing of Old Newspapers

The newspaper collector exchanges toilet paper or tissues for old newspapers and magazines. His tape-recorded refrain, a polite announcement which exalts his humble service, lets everyone know that he is driving slowly through the neighborhood.

NEWSPAPER COLLECTOR:

Maido o-najimi no chirigami kōkan-sha de gozaimasu. Furu-shinbun, furu-zasshi nado gozaimashitara, tashō ni kakawarazu koe o kakete kudasai. Kōkyū na toiretto-pēpā to o-torikae itashimasu.

This is your local wastepaper exchange truck. If you have old newspapers or magazines, no matter whether the quantity is great or small, let me know. They will be exchanged for high-quality toilet paper.

Kekko desu =
Kyomi ga arimasen node okotowari itashimasu - I have no
Maniyatte imasu = I already have it. interest

RESIDENT:

Sumimasen. O-negai shimasu.

Excuse me. I'd like to exchange this.

NEWSPAPER COLLECTOR:

Maido arigatō gozaimasu. San kiro ne. Ja, kono tisshū o dōzo.

Thank you for your patronage. That's three kilos. Please take these tissues.

RESIDENT:

Dōmo arigatō.

Thanks.

Warning Neighbors About a Party

Your neighbors will appreciate being warned that you plan to have a party and that it may be noisy.

FOREIGNER:

Konban wa.

Good evening.

NEIGHBOR:

Dōzo, dōzo.

Do come in. (*lit.*, Please, please.)

FOREIGNER:

Iya, genkan-saki de shitsurei shimasu. Jitsu wa, ashita no ban, tomo-dachi no sayōnara pātii o uchi de suru koto ni narimashita. Sukoshi urusai kamo-shiremasen. Mōshi-wake arimasen ga yoroshiku o-negai shimasu.

No, I'm fine here at the door. I've just come to tell you that I'll be giving a farewell party for a friend tomorrow evening. I hope we don't disturb you, but it may turn out to be rather noisy.

NEIGHBOR:

Iie. Otagai-sama desukara. Waza-waza dōmo.

That's all right. Next time it'll probably be us. Thanks for telling us.

FOREIGNER:

Dōzo yoroshiku.

Thank you.

Complaining About Noise

When you have to say something tactfully, try to speak hesitantly, waiting for a nod or word of agreement from the other before continuing. In this dialogue, a graduate student politely asks the neighbors to do something about a noisy dryer.

STUDENT:

Itsumo o-sewa ni natte imasu.

Thank you for always being so good to me.

NEIGHBOR:

Iie.

Not at all.

STUDENT:

Jitsu wa hijō ni ii-nikui no desu ga, otaku-sama no kansōki no oto ga gata-gata to uchi ni hibikimashite, yoku nerarenain' desu.

I don't know how to say this, but even from my apartment, I can hear your dryer clattering so much that I haven't been able to sleep.

NEIGHBOR:

A, sō desu ka?

Oh, I didn't realize.

STUDENT:

Osoku made kaki-mono o suru toki mo arimasu shi, yabun wa narubeku oto ga morenai yō ni o-negai dekinai deshō ka?

Sometimes I stay up late writing so I really would appreciate it if you would try not to make so much noise at night.

NEIGHBOR:

Hai, wakarimashita. Mōshi-wake arimasen deshita.

I see. I'm very sorry.

STUDENT:

Dōka, yoroshiku o-negai itashimasu.

Thank you very much.

Asking Someone to Move a Car

If you need to have a neighbor move a car, a quick conversation through the interphone should suffice.

MAN:

Sumimasen. Tonari no Mitcheru desu ga, o-taku no kuruma o ugoka-shite kudasaimasen ka?

Hello. This is Mitchell from next door. Would you mind moving your car?

NEIGHBOR:

Mōshi-wake arimasen. Sugu mairimasu.

I'm very sorry. I'll be right there.

Apologizing to a Neighbor

Apologies should be spoken in a quiet voice and accompanied with bows. In this dialogue, a parent apologizes for a broken window.

PARENT:

Dōmo mōshi-wake gozaimasen. Kodomo ga mado-garasu o watte shimatte, taihen go-meiwaku o kakemashita. O-kega wa arimasen deshita ka?

We're terribly sorry for all the trouble our child caused when he broke your window. Was anyone hurt?

NEIGHBOR:

Kega wa arimasen deshita yo.

No, no one was hurt.

PARENT:

Sore wa yokatta desu. Shūri-dai wa watashi no hō de haraimasu node, dōka seikyū-sho o watashi no hō ni o-mawashi kudasai. Hontō ni mōshi-wake gozaimasen deshita.

I'm glad to hear that. We'll pay for the damage so please send the repair bill to us. I really do apologize.

Reporting a Robbery

In this dialogue, a house break-in is reported to the policeman on duty at the neighborhood police box.

FOREIGNER:

Sumimasen. Matsugaoka san-chōme jū-roku-banchi no Mitcheru desu ga, sakuya dorobō ni hairarete, genkin o nusumaremashita. Dō sureba ii desu ka?

Excuse me. My name is Mitchell and I live at Matsugaoka 3–16. Last night our house was broken into and some money was stolen. What should we do?

POLICEMAN:

*Ja, koko ni o-namae, jūsho, itsu-goro hairareta to omou ka, nusumareta kingaku o kaite kudasai.   * * *   Dewa, chotto matte kudasai. Issho ni ikimasu kara.*

All right. Please fill in your name, address, the approximate time of the break-in, and the sum stolen.   * * *   Just a moment. I'll go with you to the house.

Going on Vacation

If you go on vacation, you might want to ask one of your neighbors to keep an eye on the house. This dialogue begins with a foreigner explaining why she has come to see her neighbor.

FOREIGNER:

Jitsu wa, o-negai ga arun' desu ga. Ashita kara Amerika e kaeru node, ikkagetsu rusu ni shimasu. Shujin no kaisha no denwa bangō ga koko ni kaite arimasu node, nani-ka arimashitara, go-renraku kudasaimasen ka?

Actually, I want to ask you a favor. We're leaving for the United States tomorrow and the house will be vacant for a month. This is the telephone number of my husband's office. Would you get in touch with the office if anything happens?

NEIGHBOR:

Hai, wakarimashita. Ii desu ne. Yukkuri tanoshinde kite kudasai.

Yes, I certainly will. And I hope you have a nice, relaxing time.

FOREIGNER:

Arigatō gozaimasu. Yoroshiku o-negai shimasu.

Thank you. And thanks for keeping an eye on the house.

Useful Words and Expressions

kōban	police box
chōnai-kai	town association

chōnai-kaichō	chairman of the town association
chōnai-kaihi	town association dues
kairan-ban	notice passed around the neighborhood
ie/uchi	one's own home or house
o-taku	someone else's home or house; also polite word referring to person to whom you are talking
jūkyo/jūtaku	house, housing, residence
jūtaku-chi	residential area
danchi	apartment complex
ikken-ya	solitary house (as opposed to a townhouse complex)
manshon	apartment, condominium
apāto	apartment (usually one with a comparatively inexpensive rent)
kanri-nin	caretaker
tsubo	old Japanese unit for measuring land area and floor space; equivalent to two mats, *jō* (to convert *tsubo* to square meters, multiply by 3.3)
chirigami kōkan	old newspaper collection (*lit.*, tissue exchange)
sērusu-man	salesman
oshi-uri	pushy salesman
demae	restaurant delivery
tachi-banashi o suru	stand chatting

3 The Telephone

ALTHOUGH TELEPHONING in any foreign language is difficult, it can be especially frustrating in Japanese. What can you do to improve the way you sound on the telephone? To begin with, try not to worry too much about having to use respect language. If you feel confident in honorific and humble language, by all means, you should go ahead and use it when you talk on the telephone. On the other hand, if respect language is not your forte, you should not worry. As long as you use -*san* after people's names and the *masu* form of verbs, you can be sure that no one will think the worse of you.

One easy way to improve your ability to talk on the telephone is to learn certain useful phrases. The most common telephone phrase, of course, is *Moshi-moshi* (Hello). A wonderfully expressive phrase, *Moshi-moshi* conjures up images of frustrated callers trying to get connected in the early days of the telephone. People nowadays may say *Moshi-moshi?* just to make sure that you are still there.

Another handy phrase is *Konaida wa dōmo* (Thank you for the other day). This phrase is used very frequently even when there is nothing in particular that requires thanks. *Konaida wa dōmo* and other expressions of gratitude, denial, and inquiry are usually mentioned before stating the reason for the call. Often these expressions are spoken at breakneck speed until the caller arrives at *Jitsu wa* (Well, the reason I'm calling is. . .). If you cannot match this speed, you could try to hold your own with other useful, albeit abbreviated, phrases such as *Iie, Dōmo,* and *Kochira koso.*

Finally, how should you deal with the genteel lady who, determined to have the last word, endlessly strings courtesies together at the end of the telephone call? The only way to end your conversation is to voice a slow but determined *Gomen kudasai* (Goodbye) and then to replace the receiver, regardless of whether or not you still hear talking on the other end.

Keep in mind that the more you speak Japanese on the telephone, the easier it will become. If one day you find yourself bowing while on the telephone, you will know that your Japanese is perfect!

Answering the Telephone

When you answer the telephone, it is customary to give either your name or the name of your company or department.

- *Satō desu.*

  Sato speaking.
- *Sōmuka desu.*

  General Affairs Department.

Asking for Someone

Ordinarily a person asking for someone on the telephone begins by politely giving his or her own name and organization.

- *Kinguzu Akademii no Shēfā to mōshimasu ga. Yamada Kyōju, irasshaimasu ka?*

  My name is Schaeffer and I'm with King's Academy. Is Professor Yamada in?

A person calling his own office and asking for a colleague would most likely use the ordinary *masu* form of verbs.

- *Burento desu ga. Yamada-san, o-negai shimasu.*

  This is Brent. Can I speak to Mr. Yamada?

A person calling his own office and asking for someone who is older would use respect language.

- *Burento desu ga. Tanaka Buchō, irasshaimasu ka?*

  This is Brent speaking. Is Mr. Tanaka in? (*lit.,* Is Division Manager Tanaka in?)

On the other hand, a person wishing to speak to a member of his own family would refer to him or her with the same humble terms that he would use for himself.

- *Burento desu ga, chichi (kanai/haha/musuko/musume) wa orimasu ka?*

  This is Brent. Is my father (wife/mother/son/daughter) there?

When calling someone's home late at night, most people start the conversation with an apology.

- *Yabun mōshi-wake arimasen ga.*
  Excuse me for calling this late at night.

Starting a Conversation

These phrases are often used at the start of a telephone conversation:

- *Chotto o-kiki shitain' desu ga.*
  I have an inquiry.
- *Tabi-tabi sumimasen.*
  Sorry to keep phoning you.
- *O-denwa itadaita sō desu ga.*
  I had a message saying you'd called.
- *Saki-hodo wa dōmo.*
  Thank you for just now. (This expression is used when phoning people back with the answer, for example, to an inquiry.)
- *Senjitsu wa dōmo./Konaida wa dōmo.*
  Thank you for the other day.
- *Shibaraku desu ne.*
  It's been a while, hasn't it?

Taking a Call for Someone Else

These expressions are useful when the call is for somebody else:

- *Hai, chotto matte kudasai.*
  Please wait a moment.
- *Shitsurei desu ga, dochira-sama desu ka?*
  Excuse me, but may I ask who is calling?

If the person cannot get to the telephone, say one of the following:

- *Rusu desu./Dekakete orimasu.*
  She's gone out.
- *Ima seki o hazushite imasu.*
  She's not at her desk right now.
- *Denwa-chū desu.*
  She's on another telephone.

- *Kaigi-chū desu.*
  She's in a meeting.
- *Jugyō-chū desu.*
  She's teaching./She's attending class.

Leaving a Message

If the person you wish to speak with is not in, ask if you can leave a message.

- *Denwa ga atta koto o o-tsutae kudasai. Mata o-denwa shimasu.*
  Tell him I called. I'll call back later.
- *Dengon, o-negai dekimasu ka?*
  Can I leave a message?
- *O-tesuki no toki ni, ori-kaeshi o-denwa kudasai.*
  Please ask him to call as soon as he's free.
- *Owarimashitara, watashi ni denwa o suru yō ni o-tsutae kudasai.*
  When he's through, please ask him to telephone me.

Saying Goodbye

Listed below are five different ways to say goodbye on the telephone. If you have made a request, you might want to precede the following phrases with *Yoroshiku o-negai shimasu* (*lit.*, Please favor me).

EXPRESSION: *Sayōnara.*
  USAGE: Polite, used between friends

EXPRESSION: *Ja, mata.*
  USAGE: Informal, used between friends

EXPRESSION: *Shitsurei shimasu.*
  USAGE: Polite, used especially in business situations

EXPRESSION: *Gomen kudasai.*
  USAGE: Polite, used especially by women for any occasion, and sometimes by men in business situations

EXPRESSION: *Dōzo yoroshiku.*
  USAGE: Polite, often used if a request has been made

Calling in Sick

This conversation is between two men, an English teacher and his Japanese boss. Note that the boss uses informal men's speech while the teacher uses formal speech.

BOSS:

Okada desu.

Okada speaking.

TEACHER:

Gari desu.

It's Garry.

BOSS:

Yā! Dō shita no?

Hi! What's the matter?

TEACHER:

Jitsu wa, hidoi kaze o hiite shimatte, kyō ichi-nichi yasumasete itadakitain' desu ga.

Well, I've got a terrible cold, and I'd like to take the day off.

BOSS:

Sore wa komatta na. Kyō kimi no kawari ni naru hito ga inai node, nantoka dete korarenai kana?

Oh, no. I've got no one to replace you today. Can't you somehow make it in?

TEACHER:

Netsu ga atte, chotto muri desu.

Not really. I've got a fever.

BOSS:

Sō ka. Ja, shikata nai ne. O-daiji ni.

I see. Well, it can't be helped. Take care of yourself.

TEACHER:

Mōshi-wake arimasen. Shitsurei shimasu.

I'm really sorry. Goodbye.

Making an Appointment

The language used in business can be very formal. In this dialogue, a foreign banker makes an appointment with a client. Since the banker is the one making the request, he is reserved and polite.

BANKER:

Moshi-moshi. Takahashi Buchō desu ka?

Hello? Is this Mr. Takahashi? (*lit.,* Division Manager Takahashi)

CLIENT:

Hai, sō desu.

Yes, speaking.

BANKER:

ABC Ginkō no Konāzu de gozaimasu ga, ohayō gozaimasu.

This is Connors of ABC Bank. Good morning.

CLIENT:

Ohayō gozaimasu. Itsumo o-sewa ni natte orimasu.

Good morning. (*lit.,* We're very much obliged to you.)

BANKER:

Kochira koso. Jitsu wa, Buchō-san no go-tsugō o kikimashite, aite iru jikan ni demo o-ukagai dekitara to omoimashite.

On the contrary. I'm calling because I'd like to come and see you and I was wondering when would be convenient.

CLIENT:

A sō desu ka? Go-yōken wa nan' desu ka?

I see. What is it about?

BANKER:

Hai. Watakushi-domo no ginkō no atarashii kin'yū shōhin no koto o go-setsumei ni agaritai no desu ga.

I'd like to come and tell you about our bank's new investment plan.

CLIENT:

Kekkō desu yo. Itsu-goro ga yoroshii desu ka?

All right. When would be convenient?

BANKER:

Sō desu ne. Dochira ka to iu to, ashita ka asatte, hayai hō ga iin' desu ga.

Let me see. Preferably tomorrow or the day after. The sooner the better.

CLIENT:

Ē-to, sō shimasu to, ashita no gogo nara orimasu.

Let's see. I'll be here tomorrow afternoon.

BANKER:

Sore-dewa, ashita ni-ji goro ukagatte mo yoroshii deshō ka?

Then may I come around two o'clock tomorrow?

CLIENT:

Kekkō desu. Ashita no gogo, ni-ji, o-machi shite orimasu.

That's fine. I'll be waiting for you at two tomorrow afternoon.

BANKER:

Arigatō gozaimasu. Sore-dewa, o-ukagai itashimasu. Yoroshiku o-negai shimasu. Shitsurei shimasu.

Thank you. Well then, I look forward to seeing you. Goodbye.

Changing an Appointment

Using the banker-client situation of the previous section, this dialogue shows how you can reschedule an appointment over the telephone.

BANKER:

Konāzu desu ga, saki-hodo wa dōmo arigatō gozaimashita. Jitsu wa, o-yakusoku itadaitan' desu ga, ashita kyū na yōken de Ōsaka e iku koto ni narimashite, hontō ni mōshi-wake nain' desu ga, asatte ni nobashite itadakenai deshō ka?

This is Connors again. It's about our appointment. It turns out that I have to go to Osaka tomorrow on urgent business. Would it be possible to postpone the appointment until the day after tomorrow?

Calling Directory Assistance

It is much quicker to call directory assistance (dial 104) than to try and search for a number in a telephone directory.

OPERATOR:

Bangō annai desu.

Directory assistance.

CALLER:

Moshi moshi. ABC Kōkū wa nanban deshō ka?

Hello. What number is ABC Airways?

OPERATOR:

Hai. O-machi kudasaimase. Yoyaku de yoroshii deshō ka?

One moment please. Do you want reservations?

CALLER:

Hai, yoyaku, o-negai shimasu.

Yes, reservations please.

OPERATOR:

*Dewa go-annai itashimasu. * * * O-matase itashimashita. Sono kata wa rei-san no san-hachi-ichi-ichi no nana-ichi-rei-roku desu. Arigatō gozaimashita.*

Here is the information. (recording) Sorry to have kept you waiting. The number is 03-3811-7106. Thank you.

Phoning Emergency Services

To telephone the police, dial 110. This emergency number is known as *hyaku tōban*.

For fires and situations requiring an ambulance, dial 119. You should be aware, however, that if you call 119 at night, you will not be able to choose which hospital you want to go to; if you want to be treated by a particular hospital, telephone that hospital for an ambulance or find your own way there.

In this conversation, a foreigner has just dialed 119 to call an ambulance for a friend.

FIRE/AMBULANCE SERVICE:

Kyūkyū-tai desu.

Emergencies.

FOREIGNER:

Kyūkyū-sha, o-negai shimasu.

I need an ambulance.

55

FIRE/AMBULANCE SERVICE:
Hai. Dō shimashita ka?
OK. What's happened?

FOREIGNER:
Tomodachi ga taorete, ishiki-fumei desu!
My friend's lying unconscious!

FIRE/AMBULANCE SERVICE:
Ochitsuite, o-namae to jūsho o dōzo.
Keep calm and give me your name and address.

FOREIGNER:
Supurai desu. Jūsho wa Ichigao ni no yon no san. Famiri Kōpo desu.
The name's Spry. The address is Family Co-op, Ichigao 2–4–3.

FIRE/AMBULANCE SERVICE:
Me-jirushi ni naru yō na mono o itte kudasai.
Please tell me if there are any landmarks.

FOREIGNER:
ABC Ginkō no ura desu.
We're behind the ABC Bank.

FIRE/AMBULANCE SERVICE:
Hai. Sugu ikimasu.
We'll be right there.

Of the following phrases, the first concerns the fire department, the next two, the police.

• *Ie ga kaji desu. Sugu kite kudasai.*
  The house is on fire. Come immediately.
• *Fushin na hito ga ie no mae de uro-uro shite imasu.*
  There's a suspicious person loitering in front of our house.
• *Tonari de bōryoku o furutte'ru mitai desu.*
  There seems to be a fight going on next door.

Giving Directions

In Japan, addresses refer to blocks, not to streets. The numbering of the blocks can be difficult to follow, and to confuse things even more, the numbering of the houses is often not in sequence. Detailed directions and plenty of landmarks are a great help in finding a place. The following phrases show how you can give someone directions.

- *Chika-tetsu no Chiyoda-sen ni notte, Yoyogi Kōen de orite kudasai.*
Take the Chiyoda subway line and get off at Yoyogi Park.
- *Nishi-guchi ni dete kudasai.*
Come out through the station's west exit.
- *Mitsubishi Ginkō no kado o hidari ni magatte kudasai.*
Turn left at the Mitsubishi Bank.
- *Tsuki-atari de migi ni orete, massugu ni itte kudasai.*
At the end of the road, turn right and then go straight.
- *Daigaku-mae no shingō o migi ni magatte, michi ni sotte kimasu to, hidari ni shiroi manshon ga arimasu. Sono ni-kai desu.*
Turn right at the traffic lights in front of the university and follow the road until you come to a white apartment building on the left. We're on the second floor.

Admitting You Are Lost

No matter how careful you are, it still is easy to get lost in Japan. Always try to carry the telephone number of your destination; it can be a lifesaver. In this dialogue, a lost foreigner calls his host for help.

HOST:

Fujita desu.

The Fujita residence.

GUEST:

Tomu desu. Okurete sumimasen. Michi ga wakaranakute. Ima eki ni modottan' desu.

This is Tom. I'm sorry to be late but I can't find the way. I've come back to the station.

HOST:

Eki no doko desu ka?

Whereabouts in the station are you?

GUEST:

Hai, anō, gādo no shita no yakkyoku no mae desu.

Well, I'm in front of a pharmacy that's under the railway line.

HOST:

Jā ne, ō-dōri wakarimasu ka?

Can you see the main road?

GUEST:

Hai.

Yes.

HOST:

Ō-dōri ni dete, migi no hō no saka o nobotte kite kudasai. Mukae ni dete imasu kara.

Go to the main road and start walking up the hill that's on your right. I'll come out and meet you.

GUEST:

Arigatō gozaimasu.

Thank you very much.

HOST:

Ja, nochi-hodo.

See you later.

GUEST:

O-negai shimasu.

Thank you.

Useful Telephone Numbers

This list contains some numbers you may want to keep by the telephone. The weather and time reports are tape-recorded, so if you do not catch what is said the first time around, you can listen again.

0051	KDD international operator
100	Operator
115	Telegrams
106	Collect calls
104	Directory Assistance
113	Telephone repairs
110	Police
119	Fire/ambulance service
177	Weather (or area code + 177)
117	Time

(03) 3502-1461	Tourist Information Center (T.I.C.) in Tokyo; offers assistance in English
(075) 3371-5649	Tourist Information Center (T.I.C.) in Kyoto; offers assistance in English
(03) 3264-4347	Tokyo English Lifeline; offers information and counseling in English
(03) 3201-1010	NTT English Language Information Service in Tokyo

Useful Words and Expressions

kōshū denwa	public telephone
denwa suru/denwa o kakeru	to telephone
denwa o kiru	to hang up
Denwa ga kireta.	The line has gone dead.
Denwa ga haitte imasu.	There is a telephone call (for you).
Denwa ga haitta.	There was a telephone call (for you).
Denwa ga tōi desu.	I can't hear you very well (We have a bad connection).
denwa bangō	telephone number
machigai denwa	wrong number
kyoku ban	area code
kōkan-shu	operator
rusu-ban denwa	answering machine
kokusai denwa	international call
itazura denwa	obscene/prank telephone call

4   Shopping

THE EMPHASIS PLACED on training employees helps maintain Japan's high standards of customer service. The staff's shouts of welcome and thanks given every time a customer walks in and out of an establishment have been well-practiced. In shops, hair salons, gasoline stations, and other service-related businesses, people round off their morning meetings with choral repetitions of the key phrases, *Irasshaimase, Arigatō gozaimashita,* and *Mata dōzo* (Welcome, thank you, and please come again). This service, which is practiced and implemented daily, is a sign of sheer professionalism.

Although most stores open at around 10:00 a.m., the time they close varies according to the type of store. Department stores and supermarkets usually close at around 6:30 p.m. while neighborhood stores close at around 9:00 p.m. Some stores stay open until 11:00 p.m., and convenience stores, commonplace in cities, often are open twenty-four hours. Large stores usually open on Sunday and close one other day of the week.

Bargaining is not practiced in Japan except in flea markets, secondhand stores, and large electronics and camera stores. Storekeepers instead may give discounts, hand out free gifts, slip a few extra items in the bag, or reduce the price to a round figure. Since competition in most industries is intense, you can expect a discount on large purchases like home appliances and computer products. Shop around when buying an expensive item like a car.

With the cost of living so high, how do Japanese housewives feed and clothe their families and still maintain one of the highest rates of savings in the world? One reason is motivation. Japanese need savings not only to educate their children but also to provide for illness and old age, two major areas that social welfare does not cover adequately. Another reason is that even though they spend extravagant sums on gifts and contributions to weddings and other social events, Japanese tend to be quite frugal at home. People spend five thousand yen on a melon to give as a gift, but when buying everyday items, they go out of their way to stock up on discounted goods.

Men are only too willing to relinquish to their spouses the task of managing the household budget. Fortunately, Japanese wives seem to enjoy the challenge of making the monthly salary go a long way. Usually the wife sets aside savings and social expenses and then manages with what is left for the month.

The necessities—food, housing, and electricity—are expensive. If you want to have some resources left over to enjoy the good things in life (which unfortunately are expensive too), you may have to be more careful when shopping than you would in other countries.

Buying Tangerines

The owner of a fruit shop greets everyone with a loud and hearty *Irasshai!* (Welcome!) and sends his regular customers off with an equally spirited *Maido arigatō gozaimasu!* (Thank you for patronizing the shop).

In this dialogue, the owner sells some tangerines to a young lady, one of his regular customers. After he tells her the price, he slips a couple more in the bag.

FRUIT SHOP OWNER:

Irasshai! O-jōsan, Nihon ni naremashita ka?

Welcome! Have you gotten used to Japan, young lady?

CUSTOMER:

Mada mada. Mikan kudasai. Ikura desu ka?

No, not yet. Some tangerines, please. How much are they?

FRUIT SHOP OWNER:

Yonhyaku-en. Sukoshi sābisu desu. Hyaku-en no o-tsuri. Maido!

That'll be four hundred yen. Here's a few extra for you. Your change is one hundred yen. Thank you!

Going to a Dry Cleaner

Because summers in Japan are hot and humid, clothes left in the closet may develop mildew. Most Japanese pack away off-season clothes with mothballs, *bōchū-zai*, in airtight boxes or drawers, a practice known as *koromo-gae*. Despite these precautions, you still may end up having to take some of your clothes to the dry cleaner.

DRY CLEANER:

Konnichi wa. Ii aki-bare desu ne.

Hello. Beautiful autumn weather, isn't it?

CUSTOMER:

Ē, sō desu ne. Demo natsu wa shikke ga ōkute. Mite, kono sētā. Natsu-jū hiki-dashi ni shimatte oitara, kabi-darake ni natchatta. Kirei ni narimasu ka?

Yes, it is. But it was so humid this summer. Look at these sweaters. I left them in the drawer all summer, and now they're covered with mildew. Will they come clean?

DRY CLEANER:

Yatte minai to wakaranai kedo, tabun daijōbu deshō.

I can't say until we've tried, but they'll probably be OK.

CUSTOMER:

Ikura kakaru deshō ka?

About how much will it cost?

DRY CLEANER:

Futsū wa ichi-mai yonhyaku-en desu kedo, shimi no guai ni yotte mō sukoshi kakaru kamo-shiremasen ne. Hatsuka ikō nara dekite imasu kara.

Usually it costs four hundred yen each, but it depends on the stain. It may cost a little more. They'll be ready after the twentieth.

CUSTOMER:

O-negai shimasu.

Thank you.

Ordering a Product

Many stores in Japan do not stock large quantities of goods. If you do not need the product right away, you can have the clerk order an out-of-stock item for you.

CUSTOMER:

Sumimasen. Kore no shiro, arimasu ka?

Excuse me. Do you have this in white?

CLERK:

Iro wa dete iru dake desu keredomo.

I'm afraid what colors we have are all out (on the shelves).

CUSTOMER:

Itsu hairimasu ka?

When will you get some more?

CLERK:

Chotto matte kudasai. Ichiō zaiko o tashikamete kimasu node.   * * *
Yappari kiretan' desu ga, Kin'yōbi ni mata hairimasu.

Just a moment, please. I'll go and check the stock once more.
  * * * Yes, we have run out of stock, but we'll have some
more in on Friday.

CUSTOMER:

Chūmon shite moraemasu ka?

Could I have you order one for me?

CLERK:

Hai. O-namae to denwa bangō, o-negai shimasu.

Certainly. Could I have your name and telephone number?

Going to a Photo Shop

Because many photo shops do not stock a wide variety of film, it
is a good idea to have enough rolls of the film you want to use
before you go on a trip. In this dialogue, a customer has just stepped
inside a family-run shop.

CUSTOMER:

Gomen kudasai.

Hello?

SHOPKEEPER:

Hai, hai.

Yes, may I help you? (*lit.*, Yes, yes.)

CUSTOMER:

Ribāsaru firumu, oite'masu ka?

Do you stock slide film?

SHOPKEEPER:

Chotto oite inain' desu kedo.

I'm afraid we don't stock it.

CUSTOMER:

*Sore ja, futsū no firumu o ippon kudasai. Sore ni kore o yaki-mashi shite
kudasai.*

65

Then I'll take a roll of print film. And I'd also like some reprints of these.

SHOPKEEPER:

Shirushi o tsukete iru tokoro desu ne. Wakarimashita. Yūgata made ni dekimasu node.

I see. The ones marked, right? They'll be ready this evening.

CUSTOMER:

O-negai shimasu.

Thank you.

You might also find the following expressions useful to know:

- *Kore o hiki-nobashitain' desu ga.*

  I'd like this enlarged.

- *Pasupōto-yō no shashin o totte moraitain' desu ga.*

  I'd like a passport photograph taken.

- *Kyō-jū ni dekimasu ka?*

  Will they be ready today?

- *Kyanon no shin-gata ichigan-refu kamera wa ikura de kaemasu ka?*

  How much can I buy the new Canon single-reflex camera for?

Trying on a Garment

Most stores allow you to try on clothes. You do not have to feel obligated to buy something, however, just because you tried it on.

CUSTOMER:

Kore o shichaku shite ii desu ka?

May I try this on?

SALESPERSON:

*Dōzo, kochira e. * * * Ikaga desu ka?*

Certainly. This way, please. * * * How do you like it?

CUSTOMER:

Dōmo arigatō. Mō sukoshi mite mimasu. Mata kimasu.

Thank you. I'm going to look around a bit more. I'll be back again.

SALESPERSON:

O-machi shite orimasu.

We'll be here waiting.

Additional useful expressions are listed below:

· *Saizu ga wakaranai node, hakatte kudasai.*

I don't know my size. Will you measure me?

· *Suso o naoshite moraemasu ka?*

Can you fix the hem?

Returning a Product

Stores will usually exchange an item if you have a receipt of purchase.

CUSTOMER:

Kinō kore o kattan' desu ga, sode ga mijikai node kaeshitain' desu.

I bought this yesterday but the sleeves are too short. I'd like to return it.

SALESPERSON:

Hai, wakarimashita. Shōhin-ken de o-kaeshi suru koto ni narimasu ga, yoroshii deshō ka?

That's fine. The refund will be in vouchers for the store. Is that all right?

CUSTOMER:
Kekkō desu.
That's fine.
SALESPERSON: (handing over the vouchers)
Dōzo. O-tashikame kudasai.
Here you are. Please check them.
CUSTOMER:
Sumimasen deshita.
Sorry to have troubled you.

Shopping for Shoes

Although Japanese stores often have very stylish shoes on display, you might discover that most of them are too small for you. Fortunately, this situation is changing. As the average height increases with each new generation, larger shoe sizes are beginning to appear on the market.

CUSTOMER:
Kore no nijū-yon ten-go, arimasu ka?
Do you have this in size 24.5?
ASSISTANT:
Shōshō o-machi kudasai. * * * *Dōzo, o-haki ni natte kudasai.*
One moment, please. * * * Here we are. Please try them on.
CUSTOMER:
Sukoshi kitsui desu ne. Kono ue no saizu, arimasen ka?
It's a little tight. Do you have the next larger size?
ASSISTANT:
Nijū-yon ten-go made nan' desu ga.
They only go up to 24.5.
CUSTOMER:
Sō desu ka. Nobasu koto ga dekimasu ka?
I see. Can they be stretched?
ASSISTANT:
Hai, dekimasu.
Yes, they can.
CUSTOMER:
Ja, kono atari o sukoshi nobashite kudasai.

In that case, will you please stretch them a little around this point?

Understanding Discount Terms

In Japanese, a sale is usually either *sēru* or *bāgen*. You may be urged to buy with one of these phrases:
- *O-kaidoku desu yo.*
  It's a bargain.
- *Yasuku natte orimasu.*
  It's reduced.
- *Hangaku desu.*
  It's half price.

Price reductions are expressed in percent, *pāsento,* or in units of ten percent, *wari.* "Off" in Japanese is *hiki,* which changes to *biki* when it follows either *pāsento* or *wari.* For example:
- *Juppāsento-biki desu.*
  It's ten percent off.
- *Ichiwari-biki desu.*
  It's ten percent off.
- *Sanwari-biki desu.*
  It's thirty percent off.

Bargaining Prices

In Japan, you do not usually negotiate prices except at flea markets, secondhand shops, and large electronics and camera stores.

CUSTOMER:
Konnichi wa. Kono Kutani no kabin wa ikura desu ka?
Hello. How much is this Kutani vase?

ANTIQUE DEALER:
Ichiman-en desu ne.
Ten thousand yen.

CUSTOMER:
Ichiman!
Ten thousand!

ANTIQUE DEALER:

Kore wa horidashi-mono desu.

It's a good buy.

CUSTOMER:

Demo ichiman-en wa takai. Chotto makete moraenai kana?

But ten thousand yen is too much. Can't I have it for less?

ANTIQUE DEALER:

Jā, benkyō shite, hassen-en.

OK. I'll knock it down to eight thousand yen.

CUSTOMER:

Gosen ni shite yo.

Make it five thousand.

ANTIQUE DEALER:

Iya, sore wa muri desu yo.

No, that's impossible.

CUSTOMER:

Jā, rokusen-en.

How about six thousand yen?

ANTIQUE DEALER:

Ii deshō. O-make shimashō.

All right. It's a deal.

Getting Gas

A visit to the gas station can be a pleasure rather than a chore; no self-serve pumps or halfhearted service here. As you drive in, attendants rush to greet you, and as you drive out, one of them may step into the road to stop traffic for you.

ATTENDANT:

Irasshaimase! Irasshaimase!

Welcome! Welcome!

DRIVER:

Mantan, o-negai shimasu.

Fill it up, please.

ATTENDANT:

Hai!

Yes, sir!

DRIVER:

Sore to taiya no kūki-atsu o mite, sensha mo shite kudasai.

Also, please check the air in the tires and put the car through the carwash.

ATTENDANT:

Hai, wakarimashita. Dōzo, naka de yasunde kudasai.

Certainly, sir. Please go ahead and wait inside (the office).

Complaining About Defects

The following examples show how you can describe what is wrong with a product that you just bought:

• *Shimi/Kizu ga tsuite imasu ga.*

This is stained/chipped.

• *Hibi ga haitte imasu ga.*

This is cracked.

• *Kono chiizu o kinō kattan' desu ga, furukute taberarenain' desu.*

I bought this cheese yesterday but it's so old that we can't eat it.

• *Kono wain no koruku ga kawaite ite, poro-poro shite nukenakattan' desu yo.*

The cork in this wine was so dried up that it crumbled and couldn't be pulled out.

• *Raberu no tōri sentaku shitara, chijinde shimattan' desu.*

It shrank, even though I washed it according to the instructions on the label.

• *Kono tii-shatsu o sentaku shitara, iro ga nukete sentaku-mono zenbu ga pinku ni somattan' desu.*

When I washed this T-shirt, the color ran and turned the whole wash pink.

• *Kono bideo wa kirei ni rokuga dekinain' desu.*

This video doesn't record properly.

• *Kono raji-kase wa umaku rokuon dekinain' desu.*

This radio-cassette player doesn't record very well.

• *Kaigai hōsō mo kikoeru to osshaimashita ga, dame desu.*

You had said that it could pick up overseas broadcasts, but it doesn't.

71

- *Kono sōji-ki ga kyōryoku da to osshaimashita ga, chittomo gomi o sui-komanain' desu.*
  You said this was a powerful vacuum cleaner, but it doesn't suck up dirt at all.
- *Shūri-dai ni wa hoken ga kikimasu ka?*
  Will the repairs be covered by insurance?

Generally, the clerk will offer to change the product or give a refund. If not, you can take the initiative by saying one of the following phrases:

- *Tori-kaete moraemasu ka?*
  Will you replace it?
- *Daikin o kaeshite moraemasu ka?*
  Can I have my money back?
- *Sochira no futan de shūri shite moraemasu ka?*
  Will you pay for it to be repaired?

Telephoning the Repairman

Regular customers usually get prompt attention so it is worth cultivating a good relationship with those who service the important machines in your life. When you telephone, you should give the name of the manufacturer, the serial number, and if possible, the year the appliance was made.

CUSTOMER:
Sentaku-ki ga koshō shita node, mite moraitain' desu keredomo.
My washing machine has broken down and I'd like you to come and look at it.

SERVICE ASSISTANT:
Doko no mēkā desu ka?
What is the name of the manufacturer?

CUSTOMER:
ABC no BW-yon-ichi-nana A desu.
It's a BW-417A made by ABC.

SERVICE ASSISTANT:
Donna guai desu ka?
What's the problem?

CUSTOMER:

Dassui no mae ni tomatte shimaun' desu. Haisui mo kikimasen. Deki-tara kyō-jū ni o-negai shitain' desu ga.

It stops before the spin cycle and also the water won't drain away. If possible, I'd like you to come today.

SERVICE ASSISTANT:

Hai. O-namae to go-jūsho, o-negai shimasu.

OK. Your name and address, please.

Describing Breakdowns

The following phrases should help you describe some of the most common breakdowns.

PLUMBING:

- *Toire ga tsumatte imasu.*
  The toilet's clogged.
- *Nagashi no mizu ga nagaremasen.*
  The sink won't drain.

• *Furo ga nioimasu.*
The bathtub smells.

TELEVISION:

• *Dengen wa hairimasu ga, gamen mo oto mo demasen.*
It switches on, but there's no picture or sound.

• *Gamen ga masshiro de, eizō ga demasen.*
The screen is white and there's no picture.

• *Gamen ga chira-chira shite, zatsuon ga shimasu.*
The picture jumps and the sound buzzes.

APPLIANCES:

• *Suitchi wa hairimasu ga, atatamaranain'/hienain'/mawaranain'/
desu.*
It switches on but doesn't heat/cool/go.

• *Taimā/Sāmosutatto ga kowarete imasu.*
The timer/thermostat is broken.

• *Bane ga kireta yō desu.*
The spring seems to be broken.

CARS:

• *Enjin ga burun-burun to natte, togireru kanji ga shimasu.*
The engine's running unevenly. It feels like it's jerking.

• *Haiki-gasu ga kokute, shiroi iro o shite imasu.*
The exhaust is thick and white.

• *Nenpi ga warui yō desu. Itsumo ichi-rittā de jukkiro hashitte ita no
ga nana-kiro shika hashiremasen.*
It seems to be using too much gas. It usually goes ten kilometers
to the liter, but it's only doing seven.

Being able to explain different sounds will help you describe
a breakdown to the repairman. Sounds in Japanese are usually
expressed by onomatopoeic words; e.g., in the above section
on cars, *burun-burun* describes a motor that is not running
smoothly. Some of these onomatopoeic words are given below,
but there are many, many more.

gata-gata suru	to clatter
gatan-gatan suru	to clang

gā-gā iu	to mechanically screech (also, to complain constantly)
kachi-kachi iu	to clink (metal), rattle
gishi-gishi iu	to creak
gō-gō suru	to make a loud and continuous noise

Requesting Delivery

A customer in a department store can ask for a bulky purchase to be delivered to the home. This service is often free of charge.

SALESPERSON:

Nijū-en no o-kaeshi ni narimasu.

That's twenty yen in change.

CUSTOMER:

Arigatō. Sumimasen ga, todokete itadakemasu ka?

Thank you. Can I have it delivered?

SALESPERSON:

Yoroshii desu yo. Koko ni o-namae to go-jūsho, o-negai shimasu.

Certainly. Could you please write your name and address here.

CUSTOMER:

Hai. Tsutomete imasu node, narubeku yūgata ni o-negai shitain' desu ga.

I work, so I'd like it delivered in the evening if possible.

SALESPERSON:

Ashita no roku-ji sugi ni shimasu node.

Then I'll make it for tomorrow after six.

CUSTOMER:

O-negai shimasu.

Thank you.

Ordering Kerosene

You can telephone a nearby gasoline station and have kerosene delivered to your home.

CUSTOMER:

Tōyu o todokete hoshiin' desu ga.

I'd like some kerosene delivered.

GASOLINE-STATION ATTENDANT:

Hai. Dochira-sama deshō ka?

Certainly. May I have your name, please?

CUSTOMER:

Hinode-sō nihyaku-san gōshitsu no Chen desu.

My name is Chen and I'm in room 203, Hinode Apartments.

GASOLINE-STATION ATTENDANT:

Hai. Ato sanjippun gurai de ikimasu.

OK. We'll be along in about thirty minutes.

CUSTOMER:

Yoroshiku o-negai shimasu.

Thank you.

Useful Words and Expressions

SHOPPING

o-tsukai	daily errands
kai-mono	shopping (usually in the neighborhood)
shoppingu	shopping expedition (usually to a large shopping district)
mise/shōten	shop
shōten-gai	shopping street, arcade
yakkyoku	pharmacy
saka-ya	liquor store
kome-ya	rice merchant
hana-ya	florist
niku-ya	butcher
yao-ya	vegetable store
kanamono-ya	hardware store
bunbōgu-ya	stationery store
shashin-ya	photo shop
kuriiningu-ya	dry cleaner
depāto	department store
konbiniensu sutoa	convenience store
kyaku	customer
reji	cash register
chirashi	flyer

medama shōhin	loss leader
o-tsuri	change

HOUSEHOLD EXPENSES

kakei-bo	household acounts
kakei-bo o tsukeru	to do the household accounts
chokin	savings
shoku-hi	amount spent on food
jūkyo-hi	housing expenses (mortgage, rent, repair costs)
yachin	rent
kōnetsu-hi	amount spent on gas and electricity
kōsai-hi	amount spent on gifts and entertaining
getsumatsu no pinchi	time period before payday when money becomes tight

5　Banks and Delivery Services

OPENING A BANK account in Japan is simple. After filling out a form and making an initial deposit, you will be given a bankbook to record all deposits and withdrawals. At this time, you will be asked whether or not you want a cash card, a handy item to have because it enables you to quickly make deposits and withdrawals, and pay bills without having to wait in line for a teller. Furthermore, a card can be used on the cash-card machines even after the bank has closed.

The banks also offer a bill-paying service called *furi-komi*. If, for example, you have a utility bill to pay, you can go to any major bank and have the teller wire your money to the utility company. To save you the trouble of always having to go to the bank to pay regular bills, you can have them deducted automatically from your bank account. To apply for this service, take your bills to your bank and ask an assistant or teller to help you fill out the forms for *jidō furi-komi*.

The postal service also handles savings and remittance, although like most other foreigners, you may be more interested in its more traditional mail services. Express deliveries, which cost ¥210 extra for a letter, are made every day of the year, including Sundays and holidays. If you need to send something immediately, you could inquire about a super-express service that delivers within the hour. This service is available in Tokyo.

You should be aware that small envelopes may not be accepted, envelopes larger than the standard size of up to 23.5 cm by 12 cm will be charged extra, and airmail envelopes should not be used for domestic mail. As for packages, both domestic and overseas parcels are handled at all post offices, although you must send registered parcels from a main post office.

You can send money from the post office to other parts of Japan by telegraphic money order, a method that is quick but comparatively expensive. Postal order is one alternative. Many people, however, prefer to send money by registered mail because it saves the recipient a trip to the post office. Ask at the post office for the special money envelope and insert the amount you wish to send along with a letter if you wish to include one. Seal the double envelope and initial or stamp with a name seal. Postage is calculated according to the weight and the amount you are sending; you can send up to two hundred thousand yen and you will receive full compensation if it goes astray.

All registered mail is delivered to the addressee, who either stamps with a name seal or signs for it. As with parcels that do not fit in the mailbox, the mailman will leave a notice if no one is home. Do not ignore this notice because the mail will be returned to the sender if it is not claimed within ten days. To have the mail redelivered, write in a date when you will be home to receive delivery and mail the notice back to the post office. Or you can take the notice and some form of identification to the post office and pick it up yourself.

The postal service offers very attractive cards for New Year, spring, and midsummer. New Year cards go on sale in mid-October and sell out quickly. If posted before December 20, they will be delivered all together on New Year's Day.

When you move, the post office will forward your mail free of charge for one year. Ask for change-of-address forms at the post office. Other services offered by the post office include facsimile services, a free money-transfer service to holders of postal accounts (*harai-komi*), an overseas money-transfer service, and bill-paying services.

Private delivery services, which transport all types of parcels, provide an alternative to the postal service. These delivery services are prompt, reliable, and very popular. To send a parcel, take it to a nearby *takkyū-bin* or *takuhai-bin* pick-up point. For heavy items like skis, suitcases, or golf clubs, you can call for them to be picked up from your home. The goods travel overnight and delivery within Japan usually is guaranteed to reach any address by the next day. These services are being extended to parts of Asia, Europe, and the United States.

Changing Traveler's Checks

Traveler's checks can be changed at banks, hotels, and department stores. Be sure to pronounce clearly the *e* in *kaetai* (I'd like to change) or the word may be confused with *kaitai* (I'd like to buy).

81

TRAVELER:

Toraberāzu chekku o genkin ni kaetain' desu ga.

I'd like to cash some traveler's checks.

SALESPERSON:

Hai.

OK.

TRAVELER:

Kyō no rēto wa ikura desu ka?

What's today's rate?

SALESPERSON:

Doru no kai-ne wa hyaku yonjū-en to natte orimasu.

We're buying dollars at ¥140 yen.

TRAVELER:

Mata sagatchatta! Komatta na! Kore dake kaemashō.

It's down again! Oh, no! I'll just change this much then.

SALESPERSON:

Koko ni sain, o-negai shimasu.

Please sign here.

TRAVELER:

Hai.

OK.

At the Bank

You might find the following sentences useful when you go to the bank:

• *O-kane o furi-komitain' desu ga, dono yōshi desu ka?*

I'd like to wire some money. Which form should I use?

• *Denwa-dai o jidō furi-kae ni shitain' desu ga.*

I'd like the telephone bill deducted automatically from my account.

• *Sumimasen. Kore ni kichō shite kudasai.*

Excuse me. Could you please print out my transactions in this (bank book)?

• *Sumimasen. Kono kikai no tsukai-kata o oshiete kudasai.*

Excuse me. Could you please teach me how to use this machine?

Opening a Bank Account

When you make your first deposit, the bank will show its appreciation by giving you a small gift.

CUSTOMER:

Kōza o hirakitain' desu ga.

I'd like to open an account.

TELLER:

Inkan o o-mochi deshō ka?

Do you have a name seal?

CUSTOMER:

Motte imasen keredo.

No, I don't have one.

TELLER:

Ja, sain de kekkō desu node, go-jūsho to o-namae to kyō ireru kingaku— ikura demo yoroshii desu keredo—o-kaki kudasai.

Then a signature will do. Please fill in your address, your name, and how much you will deposit today. It doesn't matter how much.

CUSTOMER:

Hai.

All right.

TELLER:

Okyaku-sama no kyasshu-kādo o tsukurimashō ka? Kyasshu-kōnā de genkin o orosu koto ga dekimasu ga.

Shall I make a cash card for you? You will be able to withdraw cash at the cash corner.

CUSTOMER:

Hai. O-negai shimasu.

Yes, please.

TELLER:

Dewa, kochira ni yon keta no anshō bangō o kinyū shite kudasai. Kādo no hō wa isshūkan naishi tōka no uchi ni go-jitaku no hō ni todoku to omoimasu.

In that case, will you please write a four-digit number here. The card will be delivered to your home within a week or ten days.

CUSTOMER:

Arigatō gozaimashita.

Thank you.

At the Post Office

The following example sentences will be useful when you go to the post office.

- *Hyaku-en kitte ni-mai kudasai.*

  Two one-hundred-yen stamps, please.

- *Kansei-hagaki jū-mai to earoguramu san-mai o kudasai.*

  Ten stamped postcards and three aerogrammes, please.

- *Amerika made no e-hagaki wa kōkū-bin de ikura desu ka?*

  How much is it to send a postcard to America by airmail?

- *Kore wa sumōru paketto de ikimasu ka?*

  Will this go at the small-packet rate?

Sending Christmas Cards

The post office charges extra for envelopes larger than 12 cm by 23.5 cm. You should keep this in mind when sending Christmas cards.

In this dialogue, a customer has a stack of Christmas cards. Because the envelopes are unsealed, they can go at the cheaper printed-matter rate.

CUSTOMER:

Kore o insatsu-butsu to shite okuritain' desu ga.

I'd like to send these at the printed-matter rate.

CLERK:
 Ha?
 Pardon?
CUSTOMER:
 Kurisumasu-kādo desu. Ura o akete oku to insatsu-butsu to shite yasuku okureru hazu desu ga.
 They're Christmas cards. If I leave them unsealed, I should be able to send them at the cheaper printed-matter rate.
CLERK:
 Tegami ga haitte imasen ka?
 Are there any letters inside?
CUSTOMER:
 Iie. Messēji dake desu.
 No. Only messages.
CLERK:
 Chotto misete kudasai. Minna onaji desu ka?
 Can I take a look? Are they all the same?
CUSTOMER:
 Hai. Kōkū-bin de o-negai shimasu. Kurisumasu ni ma-ni-aimasu ka?
 Yes, they are. I'd like to send them by air. Will they be in time for Christmas?
CLERK:
 Hai. Daijōbu desu.
 Yes. No problem.

Mailing Money

At the post office, you can get a special envelope for sending cash. Insert the money, fill in the address, seal the envelope, and hand it to the postal clerk.
CUSTOMER:
 Genkin kakitome no fūtō o ichi-mai kudasai.
 One registered money-mail envelope, please.
CLERK:
 Hai. Dōzo.
 OK. Here you are.

* * *

CUSTOMER:
Sokutatsu de, o-negai shimasu.
By express delivery, please.

CLERK:
Ikura haitte imasu ka?
How much is in it?

CUSTOMER:
Gosen hyaku kyūjū-en desu.
There's ¥5,190.

CLERK:
Roppyaku jū-en ni narimasu ne. Dashite okimasu kara.
That'll be ¥610. I'll mail it from here.

CUSTOMER:
Arigatō gozaimasu.
Thank you.

Wiring Money Abroad

This service is available from main post offices only. The charge, which rises with the amount that is remitted, is the same for all countries.

CUSTOMER:
Gaikoku kawase no yōshi, o-negai shimasu.
May I have a foreign-exchange form, please.

CLERK:
Okuru hō?
For a remittance?

CUSTOMER:
Hai. * * * *Kono hen ga yoku wakaranain' desu kedo.*
Yes. * * * I'm not quite sure that I understand this part (of the form).

CLERK:
Ē-to, doko desu ka? Amerika-ate ni wa futsū atsukai shika dekimasen node, kore wa ii desu. Gojū-doru desu ne.
Let's see where you are sending it. There's only ordinary handling service available for the U.S., so this doesn't matter. It's for fifty dollars, right?

CUSTOMER:
   Hai, sō desu. Ikura ni narimasu ka?
   Yes, that's right. How much will it cost?

CLERK:
   Tesū-ryō wa happyaku-en de, zenbu de nanasen sanbyaku-en ni narimasu.
   The handling charge is ¥800 and the total charge is ¥7,300.

Private Delivery Services

An alternative to sending parcels through the post office is to use a private delivery service. In this dialogue, a traveler wants to do some sightseeing before catching the train back to Tokyo, so he decides to have his luggage delivered home.

TRAVELER:
   Chikaku ni takkyū-bin o daseru tokoro ga arimasu ka?
   Is there a delivery service (collection point) nearby?

HOTEL RECEPTIONIST:
   Hai, baiten ni gozaimasu.
   Yes, there's one in the hotel shop.

* * *

TRAVELER:
   Kono ni-motsu o Tōkyō no jitaku e okuritain' desu ga.
   I'd like to send this luggage to my home in Tokyo.

HOTEL SHOP ASSISTANT:
   Hai. Tōkyō wa ni-motsu hitotsu ni tsuki happyaku-en ni narimasu ne.
   Soshite fukuro ga hyaku gojū-en ni narimasu ga.
   Fine. For Tokyo, it's eight hundred yen per bag. The (protective) bags are one hundred and fifty yen each.

TRAVELER:
   Sore ja, hitotsu ni matomete ii desu ka?
   Then can I put everything in one bag?

HOTEL SHOP ASSISTANT:
   Sō desu ne.
   That's fine.

TRAVELER:
   Ashita tsukimasu ka?
   Will it arrive tomorrow?

HOTEL SHOP ASSISTANT:
Hai, tsukimasu.
Yes, it'll get there.
TRAVELER:
Sore-dewa, yoroshiku.
Fine. Thank you.
HOTEL SHOP ASSISTANT:
Arigatō gozaimashita.
Thank you.

Useful Words and Expressions

FOREIGN EXCHANGE

gaika ryō-gae	foreign exchange
kawase rēto	exchange rate
tsūka	currency
tesū-ryō	commission, handling fee
en ni kansan suru	to convert into yen
doru o kaeru	to exchange dollars
toraberāzu chekku	traveler's check

BANK

ginkō	bank
yokin	deposit
yokin suru	to make a deposit
kane o orosu	to make a withdrawal
futsū kōza	current account
teiki yokin	time deposit
tsumi-tate yokin	installment-savings account
yokin tsūchō	bankbook
sōkin/furi-komi	remittance, bank transfer
jidō furikomi	automatic remittance
yūshi/rōn	loan
riritsu	interest
inkan/hanko	name seal
yōshi	application form

POST OFFICE

yūbin-kyoku	post office

posuto	mailbox
kitte	stamp
kinen kitte	commemorative stamps
tegami	letter
kansei hagaki	prestamped postcard
nenga-jō	New Year postcard
shochū-mimai hagaki	midsummer card
sakura mēru	spring card
earoguramu	aerogramme
ko-zutsumi	parcel; small package
sumōru paketto	small package (in speech only)
kogata hōsō-butsu	small package (on forms)
insatsu-butsu	printed matter
kōkū-bin	airmail
funa-bin	seamail
kakitome	registered mail
sokutatsu	express mail
genkin kakitome	money sent by registered mail
tenkyo todoke	change-of-address card
Kurisumasu mēru no sashi-dashi kigen	last mailing date for Christmas
denshi yūbin	post-office facsimile

6 Business

LET US SUPPOSE you are about to go to your first formal business engagement in Japan and you want to know how you should prepare for it. For one thing, make sure you have business cards showing your company or affiliation. Have a few general comments ready in Japanese, perhaps concerning the weather or a recent major news event. Also be sure to dress neatly; in Japan, that means suit and tie for men, and a skirt, blouse, and jacket combination for women.

Give yourself ample time to find your destination and to have a few spare minutes to check your appearance. During this time, you can also make sure that your business cards are ready to present; needless to say, you do not want to ruin a first impression by feverishly searching in your pockets or handbag for your card.

The card-exchanging ceremony, for ceremony it is, often takes place after you are shown into the reception or meeting room. When offering your card, present it so that your name is not upside down as it faces the recipient. At the same time, bow and say your name. When the person hands you his or her card, bow and receive it with both hands, not with just one hand. If you wish, you can open the conversation by asking about the readings of the characters in the name or commenting about the person's title or department.

You can address an executive by attaching *san* to his or her title, but if you want to keep things simple, you can just address a business associate like anyone else, e.g., name plus *san*. In other words, either *Buchō-san* or *Kobayashi-san* is appropriate. *Kobayashi Buchō* also is acceptable, but combining name, title, and *san*, like *Kobayashi Buchō-san* is incorrect.

Ideally, you should use respect language throughout a business meeting, but no one will think worse of you if you slip into neutral language using the *masu* forms of verbs after the initial civilities are through. At the end of a meeting, you will leave a good final impression if you use the polite set expressions to thank your hosts for their time and to say goodbye.

Foreign businessmen in Japan may discover that much of their time is devoted to nurturing relationships with people both inside and outside the company. Colleagues within the company often go drinking after work and before the long commute home. Middle managers and people in sales entertain clients not at business lunches but at evening engagements. Golf, which is usually played with business acquaintances and rarely with friends, may take up the weekends.

Furthermore, relationships are reinforced by the *aisatsu* (courtesy call), a short visit to a client, customer, or anyone else connected with work. During the last weeks in December and again in the first weeks of January, people make their courtesy calls to thank others for what has happened during the past year and to express hope that relationships will continue through the new year. Courtesy calls are also made during the year, especially when people change positions or companies, or when new business deals have been settled.

Establishing and maintaining business relations can take a considerable amount of time, but from a business point of view, it is time well spent. The trick is to build up these relationships efficiently without taking away too much time from your personal life.

Visiting a Client's Office

When you visit someone on business in Japan, you should arrive a couple minutes early and make yourself known to the receptionist.

Tono-sama Shōbai
"Feudal Lord's Business"

This term describes a businessman who expects his product to sell itself. In recent years, *tono-sama shōbai* has been used to refer to foreign firms that do not try hard enough to sell their products in Japan's competitive market.

BUSINESSMAN:

ABC Ginkō no Mitcheru to mōshimasu ga, zaimu no Takahashi-san, irasshaimasu ka? Gogo ni-ji no o-yakusoku o itadaite orimasu ga.

My name is Mitchell and I'm from the ABC Bank. Is Mr. Takahashi from the finance department in? I have an appointment at 2:00 p.m.

RECEPTIONIST:

Shōshō o-machi kudasai. O-meishi o itadakemasu ka?

One moment please. May I have your card?

BUSINESSMAN:

Hai, dōzo.

Yes, here you are.

RECEPTIONIST: (after telephoning)

Ni-kai no hō ni dōzo.

Please go ahead to the second floor.

* * *

CLIENT:

Mitcheru-san desu ka? O-machi shite orimashita. Takahashi desu.

Ah, Mr. Mitchell? I've been expecting you. I am Takahashi.

BUSINESSMAN:

Hajimemashite. Mitcheru desu. Kyō wa o-isogashii tokoro o arigatō gozaimasu.

How do you do? My name is Mitchell. Thank you for making time to see me today.

CLIENT:

Iie, tonde-mo gozaimasen. Kochira e dōzo.

Not at all. Please come this way.

Introducing People

In the following conversation, a researcher introduces his senior colleagues in order of rank to the chairman of a Japanese company.

RESEARCHER:

Nihon daihyō no Mitcheru de gozaimasu.

This is Mr. Mitchell, our representative in Japan.

CHAIRMAN:

Hajimemashite. Miya de gozaimasu. Dōzo yoroshiku.

How do you do? My name is Miya. Pleased to meet you.

MR. MITCHELL:

Dōzo yoroshiku.

Pleased to meet you.

RESEARCHER:

Sore-kara, kochira ga fuku-buchō no Adamuzu desu. Hikari faibā no supeshiarisuto de gozaimasu.

And this is Mr. Adams, our deputy director. He's a specialist in fiber optics.

MR. ADAMS:

Dōzo yoroshiku.

Glad to meet you.

CHAIRMAN:

Dōzo yoroshiku.

I'm pleased to meet you.

RESEARCHER:

Watashi wa kenkyū-in no Sumisu de gozaimasu. Dōzo yoroshiku o-negai shimasu.

My name is Smith and I'm a researcher. It's my pleasure to meet you.

CHAIRMAN:

Kochira koso. Dewa, go-shōkai shimasu. Kochira wa senmu no Ko-bayashi desu. Sore-kara, kenkyū kaihatsu buchō no Ariake desu. Ima tantō no mono mo yobimasu node, dōzo, o-kake kudasai.

It is our pleasure as well. Now let me introduce our side. This is Mr. Kobayashi, our senior managing director. And Mr. Ariake, the director of our research and development department. I'll also call in the person who is working on this project. Please sit down.

Meeting with a Client

As in most other countries in the world, a meeting in Japan will often begin with polite small talk before proceeding to business matters.

SALESMAN:

Watashi wa mae ni ABC no Rarii kenkyū-jo ni imashita ga, jōmu wa Nōsu Karoraina wa go-zonji desu ka?

I used to be with ABC's research institute in Raleigh. Are you familiar with North Carolina?

CLIENT:

Ē. "Risāchi Toraianguru" o kengaku shita koto ga arimasu yo.

Yes. I've visited the "Research Triangle."

SALESMAN:

Sō desu ka? Itsu-goro irasshitan' desu ka?

Really? When did you go?

CLIENT:

Jū-nen mae ni narimasu ka ne.

Let's see. About ten years ago.

SALESMAN:

Chōdo ABC mo pasokon ni chikara o ire-dashita koro desu ne. Sono-go no pasokon no fukyū wa taihen na mono desu.

That was about the time ABC started concentrating on personal computers. Since then, personal computers have really come a long way.

CLIENT:

Sō desu ne. Ichijirushii hatten desu ne. De, kyō wa nani-ka?

Yes, indeed. Their progress has been remarkable, hasn't it? Now then, what can I do for you today?

SALESMAN:

Jitsu wa, atarashii seihin no go-shōkai ni agarimashita.

Well, I've come to tell you about our new product.

Kaban-mochi
"Bag-carrier"

The *kaban-mochi* is the person who does all the hard work but is actually only second in command. *Watashi wa kaban-mochi desukara* is an expression meaning that the speaker does not have the authority to make final decisions.

Starting a Conversation

These general remarks can be used to start a conversation.

• *Atsui hi ga tsuzukimasu ne.*

This hot weather doesn't let up, does it?

• *Ii o-shimeri desu ne.*

It's a welcome drop of rain, isn't it?

• *Senjitsu shinbun de, onsha ga kondo Denbā ni kōjō o tsukuru to iu kiji o mimashita ga, masu-masu o-sakan desu ne.*

I saw in the newspaper that your company is going to build a plant in Denver. Your company is doing very well, isn't it?

• *Konaida, shinbun de haiken shimashita ga.*

I read about you in the newspaper the other day.

• *O-taku no yakyū chiimu wa konogoro katsuyaku shite imasu ne.*

Your company baseball team has been doing pretty well recently, hasn't it?

• *Jōmu wa Amerika e irasshita koto ga arimasu ka?*

Have you been to the States? (speaking to a managing director)

Below are comments that will direct the conversation toward the business on hand.

• *Bijinesu wa ikaga desu ka?*

How's business?

• *Gyōkai no keiki wa ikaga desu ka?*

What's the situation like in your line of business?

• *Urete imasu ka?*

How are sales?

• *Uchi mo hidokatta desu yo.*

It has been terrible for us too.

• *Gen'yu ga neage saresō desu ga, o-taku e no eikyō wa dō desu ka?*

It looks as if the price of oil will go up. How will that affect you?

• *Kyō mo mata kawase wa en-daka/en-yasu ni ugokimashita ne.*

The yen's stronger/weaker again today.

• *Saikin no en-daka no eikyō wa dō deshō?*

What effects do you think the recent rise in the yen will have?

97

Year-end Courtesy Call (1)

During the latter half of December, sales and management personnel make year-end calls to thank clients for their business during the year. This dialogue gives examples of the typical expressions that are exchanged during such a visit.

BUSINESSMAN:

Kotoshi wa iro-iro to o-sewa ni narimashite, arigatō gozaimashita. Rainen mo yoroshiku o-negai itashimasu.

Thank you for all your help this year. We look forward to working with you next year as well.

CLIENT:

Sore wa dōmo waza-waza arigatō gozaimasu. Kochira koso iro-iro to o-sewa ni narimashita. Dōzo kochira e.

Thank you for taking the trouble to visit us. We are the ones who should be thanking you for your help. Please come this way.

* * *

CLIENT: (as guests leave)

Waza-waza go-teinei ni arigatō gozaimashita. Dōzo, yoi o-toshi o.

Thank you for visiting. Have a happy New Year.

BUSINESSMAN:

Arigatō gozaimasu. Mina-san mo yoi o-toshi o o-mukae kudasai. Rainen mo yoroshiku o-negai itashimasu.

Thank you. Happy New Year to all of you too. We look forward to continuing our relationship with you next year.

Year-end Courtesy Call (2)

Year-end courtesy calls, which can be made without an appointment, provide excellent opportunities for meeting people. The only difficulty may be that the people you go to see are out doing their rounds! If this happens, leave your card and proceed to your next destination.

BUSINESSMAN:

ABC Ginkō no Mitcheru desu ga nenmatsu no go-aisatsu ni ukagaimashita. Takahashi Buchō wa irasshaimasu deshō ka?

I'm Mitchell and I'm from ABC Bank. I've come to make a year-end call. Is Mr. Takahashi, the general manager, in?

SECRETARY:

Ainiku Takahashi wa ima gaishutsu-chū desu.

I'm afraid he is out right now.

BUSINESSMAN:

Sore-dewa, meishi o Buchō-san ni o-watashi itadakemasu ka? Kotoshi wa iro-iro to o-sewa ni narimashita. ABC Ginkō no Mitcheru ga nenmatsu no aisatsu ni ukagaimashita to o-tsutae kudasai.

Then would you give him my card? I wanted to thank him for all his help this year. Please tell him that Mitchell from ABC Bank came to see him.

SECRETARY:

Kashikomarimashita. Waza-waza arigatō gozaimashita.

Yes, I will. Thank you for calling.

New Year Courtesy Call

New Year courtesy calls should be made within the first two weeks after returning to work.

BUSINESSMAN:

Akemashite omedetō gozaimasu. Kyūnen-chū wa iro-iro to o-sewa ni narimashite, arigatō gozaimashita. Honnen mo yoroshiku o-negai itashimasu.

Happy New Year. We would like to thank you for all your help last year. We look forward to working with you this year as well.

CLIENT:

Akemashite omedetō gozaimasu. Kochira koso honnen mo yoroshiku o-negai itashimasu.

Happy New Year. We are the ones who look forward to the relationship continuing through this year.

BUSINESSMAN:

O-shōgatsu wa ikaga deshita ka?

How was your New Year?

CLIENT:

Mattaku no ne-shōgatsu de, doko e mo dekakemasen deshita.

We had a quiet New Year's holiday and didn't go anywhere.

BUSINESSMAN:

A sō desu ka? Tokoro de, kotoshi no keiki wa dō deshō ne?

I see. By the way, I wonder what kind of year it will be?

CLIENT:

Ii toshi de atte hoshii mono desu ne.

I hope it's a good year.

BUSINESSMAN:

Watakushi-domo to no tori-hiki ga fueru to iin' desu ga ne.

I hope that this year your company will continue doing more and more business with our company.

CLIENT:

Mochiron sō negaitai desu ne.

Of course, we hope so too.

BUSINESSMAN:

Sore-dewa, o-isogashii tokoro o arigatō gozaimashita.

Thank you for giving up your time to see me today.

CLIENT:

Iie. Waza-waza arigatō gozaimashita.

Not at all. Thank you for coming.

BUSINESSMAN:

Sore-dewa, kore de shitsurei shimasu.

Well, if you'll excuse me, I should be going now.

Introducing a Successor

People will appreciate it if you call on them when you change jobs or positions. If you introduce your successor at the same time, you will also ease his transition into his new job.

BUSINESSMAN:

Kondo hongoku ni kaeru koto ni narimashita. Zainichi-chū wa iro-iro to o-sewa ni narimashite, arigatō gozaimashita.

I'll soon be returning back home (to my country). Thank you for all your help while I've been in Japan.

CLIENT:

Sorewa-sorewa. De, dochira e?

I see. And where are you moving to?

BUSINESSMAN:

Watakushi wa Nyū Yōku no honsha ni modorimasu ga, kyō wa watashi no kōnin no Jonson no go-shōkai ni ukagaimashita. Watakushi dōyō yoroshiku o-negai shimasu.

I'll be returning to the head office in New York. I've called today to introduce my successor, Mr. Johnson. I hope you will be as kind to him as you have been to me.

CLIENT:

Hajimemashite. Takahashi desu.

How do you do? My name is Takahashi.

SUCCESSOR:

Shōken-bu no Jonson desu. Fiirudo no kōnin to shite mairimashita. Dōzo yoroshiku.

I'm Johnson from our securities department and I've come as Field's successor. Glad to meet you.

CLIENT:

Ima made dō iu o-shigoto o nasatte ita no desu ka?

What work were you doing before you came here?

SUCCESSOR:

Amerika honsha no Kyokutō tantō jichō o shite imashita.

I was deputy director of the Far East department in the head office.

* * *

Madogiwa-zoku
"Group by the Window'

Middle managers who have been passed over and shunted into low priority jobs or departments are referred to by this term. *Madogiwa-zoku* was coined because in a usual office setup, those nearest the windows are those who are furthest from the action.

101

BUSINESSMAN: (when leaving)

Iro-iro arigatō gozaimashita. Hayashi Shachō ni mo yoroshiku o-tsutae kudasai.

Thank you for everything. Please give my regards to the president, Mr. Hayashi.

CLIENT:

Hai, wakarimashita. O-karada o taisetsu ni. Nihon ni koraretara mata o-yori kudasai. Itsu-demo kangei shimasu.

Yes, I will. Please take care of yourself and when you visit Japan, come in and see us again. You're always welcome.

Seniority in a Company

A senior managing director, managing director, and, in a large corporation, even a director may have the authority of a vice-president in a U.S. company. The word *torishimari-yaku* before the title means that the person is a board member. Following is a list of titles given in order of seniority:

kaichō	chairman
shachō	chief executive officer, president
fuku-shachō	executive vice-president
senmu	senior managing director
jōmu	managing director
buchō	director
jichō	senior manager
kachō	manager
shunin	supervisor
kakarichō	supervisor

Below are titles for people who work at an English-conversation school:

ei-kaiwa gakkō daihyō	director (and presumably owner) of an English-conversation school
ei-kaiwa kyōshitsu shunin	head teacher of an English conversation school
ei-kaiwa kōshi/kyōshi	teacher of English conversation

Useful Words and Expressions

tori-hiki	business, transactions, dealings
keiei	management
meishi	business card
aisatsu	courtesy call
ōsetsu-shitsu	reception room
kaigi	meeting
hisho	secretary
nenmatsu no go-aisatsu	year-end courtesy call
nenshi no go-aisatsu	New Year courtesy call
nagai tsuki-ai	long-standing relationship
kōshō	negotiations
kōshō suru	to negotiate
ne-biki suru	to discount
hinshitsu	quality
patento/tokkyo	patent
bōeki shūshi	trade balance
bōeki masatsu	trade dispute
akaji	deficit, in the red
kuroji	surplus, in the black
kawase rēto	exchange rate
tōshi	investment
setsubi tōshi	capital spending
zeikin	tax
zenki	last fiscal year
konki	this fiscal year
raiki	next fiscal year

7   Traveling

WHAT IS THE best way to travel in Japan? Many Japanese travel by train because it is fast, easy, and reliable. Traveling by car is cheaper but the going can be slow, especially during weekends and holidays, when roads and expressways become extremely congested. For long trips, traveling by a combination of trains, airplanes, and rental cars can be convenient. In fact, travel agents offer special car-and-train package deals called *rēru ando renta-kā*. Another option if you travel between Tokyo and Hokkaido or Kyushu is to take advantage of special overnight trains that transport both car and passenger. Ferries also provide a way to get you and your car to distant destinations.

Visitors with tourist visas can buy special rail passes that are good for unlimited travel on the Japan Railways (JR) for periods of one, two, or three weeks. Not only do the passes provide an excellent saving, they also dispense with the troublesome task of buying tickets. Because these rail passes can not be purchased in Japan, you should ask your local travel agent for more information about them before you leave home.

If you do not have a rail pass, you will need to become familiar with buying tickets and making reservations. First, let us quickly look at the types of train tickets. The passenger ticket (*jōsha-ken*) is all you need to travel on subways, commuter trains, and, in rural regions, nonexpress trains. However, if you travel long distance on express trains like the bullet trains, you also need to buy an "express" ticket (*tokkyū-ken*). With these two tickets, the passenger and express tickets, you board the cars marked *jiyū-seki* (unreserved) and sit in any available seat.

You can also reserve seats on an express train at larger travel agents or at ticket offices in the station. For JR trains, these offices, which are known as *Midori no Mado-guchi,* are usually located near the ticket gates. Reservations, which require a reservation fee of about five hundred yen depending on the season and the type of train, can be made as far as one month in advance. To travel in luxury, you can ride in the "green car," but seats in this first-class car require a surcharge which is almost as much as the express ticket. Nonsmoking seats are available in both the reserved and unreserved sections; if you make seat reservations, be sure to specify whether you want a smoking or nonsmoking seat.

In your own country, you may be used to traveling without reserving accommodations, but in Japan you are well-advised to book in advance. Sightseers crowd the tourist areas throughout the year, and huge groups of schoolchildren tour the famous sights in spring and fall. Especially when the cherry blossoms bloom or when the autumn leaves reach their peak colors, accommodations even for weekdays may be hard to find in popular tourist places like Kyoto.

If you like traditional accommodations, you can stay at a *ryokan,* a Japanese inn where you sleep on *futon* bedding laid out on the *tatami* mats after dinner. As a rule, breakfast and dinner are included in the price, which is calculated per person. During crowded periods, rooms may not be available for single occupation.

A *minshuku,* a cheaper alternative to the *ryokan,* is a family-run guesthouse. Some *minshuku* have ten or more rooms with large communal baths, others just an extra room in an ordinary home. The breakfast and dinner, usually Japanese-style, that is served at a *minshuku* is less fancy than the elaborate food offered in the *ryokan.*

Similar to the *minshuku* is the *penshon.* These small guesthouses are often run by young couples who have fled the city to live in the country. Sleeping often is in beds, and dinner and breakfast are usually Western-style. The word *penshon,* incidentally, derives from the French word "pension."

There are still other types of accommodations you may wish to investigate. Does your company or an organization you belong to have a country lodge for its employees or members? If so, you can save money by staying there. If not, perhaps the company or organization can arrange a discount at another place.

Another option is the business hotel. Although lacking in character, business hotels provide a clean bed at a reasonable price. Furthermore, because meals are not included, business hotels offer you more flexibility to schedule your time. Not much has to be said about regular hotels in Japan, other than that they are more elegant than business hotels, as well as more expensive.

You might be intrigued with the idea of staying at one of the many temples nationwide that allow a traveler to stay overnight. Besides offering a unique look at Buddhist life, these temples often are oases of quiet. Some temples specialize in serving the delicious and nutritious temple cuisine, although others may offer a very simple meal.

And finally, there are always youth hostels and national hostels. Rates for hostels are usually very reasonable, but you might have to apply in writing well in advance.

"A change is as good as a rest" goes the saying, and this you should keep in mind as you travel in Japan. Expect the unexpected, and you will be able to enjoy your trip more.

Riding Subways and Trains

If you cannot read the fare tables for riding subways or commuter trains, buy the cheapest ticket and pay the difference at the fare adjustment window when you reach your destination. Ask for the platform you want like this:

• *Sumimasen. Shinjuku-yuki wa nanban-sen desu ka?*
Excuse me. From what platform can I get the train headed for Shinjuku?

On the platform, to make sure you are waiting for the right train, you can go up to a passenger or a station official and ask:

• *Ochanomizu de tomarimasu ka?*
Does this train stop at Ochanomizu?

When you reach your stop in a crowded train, push your way to the exit while saying:

• *Sumimasen. Orimasu.*
Excuse me. I'm getting off.

Buying Express Train Tickets

For long-distance express trains, tickets for unreserved seats often can be bought at ticket machines. However, tickets for reserved seats usually must be purchased at a ticket office.

TRAVELER:

Tsugi no Hikari de Tōkyō made ichi-mai kudasai.

One ticket to Tokyo on the next Hikari bullet train, please.

TICKET SELLER:

Man'in desu ne. Nijū-rop-pun nara seki ga arimasu ga.

The train's full. But there are seats on the (train leaving at) twenty-six minutes past.

TRAVELER:

Jā, o-negai shimasu.

OK. I'll take that.

TICKET SELLER:

Jōsha-ken mo?

Do you want a passenger ticket as well?

TRAVELER:

Hai.

Yes.

TICKET SELLER:

Gosen roppyaku-en desu.

That will be 5,600 yen.

TRAVELER:

Arigatō.

Thanks.

Types of Train Tickets

When traveling long distances, ask about ticket reductions. You may find that you get a discount if you buy a round-trip ticket rather than two one-way tickets.

The following list introduces some of the more common types of tickets and passes.

- *jōsha-ken* passenger ticket

  Charge based on the distance traveled.
- *tokkyū-ken* express ticket

  Surcharge based on type of train and distance traveled.
- *shiteiseki-ken* ticket for reserved seat

  Surcharge based on season and type of train. Usually about five hundred yen.

- *shūyū-ken* rail pass to a part of Japan
  Pass offering unlimited travel within a certain period.
- *teiki* commuting pass
  Pass offering unlimited travel for one, three, or six months.
- *kaisū-ken* coupon ticket for subways
  Eleven tickets for the price of ten.

Making a Train Reservation

To make a train reservation, consult the train timetable and fill in an application form. A travel agent or railway booking clerk, if he is not too busy, will do this for you. Preschoolers travel free of charge, and those under twelve travel at half price.

TRAVELER:

Yoyaku shitain' desu ga, ashita no asa, hachi-ji go-fun no Hikari de, otona futari ni kodomo hitori. Ōsaka made o-negai shimasu. Soshite, kin'enseki, o-negai shimasu.

I'd like to make reservations for tomorrow morning on the 8:05 Hikari bullet train for two adults and one child to Osaka. I'd like nonsmoking seats, please.

CLERK:

Hai. Nijūroku-nichi, otona futari ni kodomo hitori desu ne. Kaeri no kippu wa dō shimasu ka?

I see. Two adults and one child for the twenty-sixth. What about the return tickets?

TRAVELER:

Mada kaeri no jikan ga wakarimasen node, jiyū-seki ni shite kudasai.

We don't know yet what time we'll be coming back, so please make the return tickets for unreserved seats.

CLERK:

Hai, wakarimashita.

OK, I will.

Canceling a Train Reservation

In most cases, you will not be charged for canceling a reservation if you do it at least two days before the train leaves.

• *Jūichi-nichi, gozen ku-ji san-pun no Morioka-yuki no Yamabiko o yoyaku shitan' desu ga, sore o kyanseru shitain' desu.*
I have reservations for the Yamabiko bullet train on the eleventh at 9:03 a.m., but I'd like to cancel it.
• *Yoyaku o kyanseru shitain' desu ga, harai-modoshi ga dekimasu ka?*
I'd like to cancel my reservation. Can I get a refund?

Missing a Train

If you miss your train, ask a station official if you can ride the next train.
• *Ressha ni nori-okurete shimaimashita ga, kono kippu de tsugi no ni noremasu ka?*
I missed the train. Can I go on the next train with these tickets?

On the Train

Once you have boarded a train, these phrases will help you find a seat and get you something to eat and drink.
• *Aite'masu ka?*
Is this seat free?
• *Sumimasen. Kōhii to bentō, o-negai shimasu.*
Excuse me. Coffee and a box lunch, please.
• *O-cha kudasai.*
Green tea, please.
• *Nani bentō ga arimasu ka?*
What kind of box lunches do you have?

Besides box-lunches featuring specialties of individual stations, *ekiben*, the following selection is usually available on trains and at stations:
• *maku-no-uchi bentō* a selection of fish, meat, and vegetables with rice
• *yaki-niku bentō* grilled meat and rice
• *ton-katsu bentō* pork cutlet, shredded cabbage, and rice
• *unagi bentō* grilled eel and rice
• *sushi* sushi

Asking for Road Directions

Secondary roads are not always marked on road maps, and signs tend to be inadequate, incomprehensible, or lost in a jungle of wires, posts, placards, and shrubbery. If you get lost, you may have to ask for directions.

DRIVER:

Sumimasen. Chūō Kōsoku no iriguchi e wa kore de iin' desu ka?

Excuse me. Is this the way to the Chuo Expressway?

PASSERBY:

Iya. Iki-sugi desu ne. Temae no ōkina kōsaten ni modotte, migi e magari, soko kara san-kiro gurai ikeba kōsoku no iriguchi ga arimasu.

No. You've gone too far. Go back to the last big intersection and turn right. About three kilometers from there, you'll come to the entrance of the expressway.

DRIVER:

Arigatō gozaimashita.

Thank you very much.

Calling JAF

A modest annual fee is all you need to become a member of the Japan Automobile Federation (JAF), a nationwide organization that takes care of unexpected car trouble. JAF also offers discounts on car rentals and accommodations and gives advice on route planning.

JAF OFFICE:

Hai. Yamagata Jaffu desu.

Hello. This is JAF, Yamagata.

DRIVER:

Sukii-jō de batterii ga agatte shimattan' desu kedo, kite itadakemasu ka?

My car battery's gone dead at the ski slope. Can someone come out?

JAF OFFICE:

Hai. O-namae to basho to kaiin bangō, o-negai shimasu.

OK. Please give me your name, your location, and your membership number.

DRIVER:

Basho wa Zaō sukii-jō no chūsha-jō no iriguchi de, namae wa Uiruson, kaiin bangō wa ichi-zero-nana-san-kyū desu.

I'm at the entrance to the parking lot of the Zao ski slope, the name is Wilson, and my membership number is 10739.

JAF OFFICE:

Hai, wakarimashita. Nijippun gurai kakaru to omoimasu.

I see. It'll take about twenty minutes (to get there).

DRIVER:

Sore-dewa, o-negai shimasu.

OK. Thank you.

Describing Car Breakdowns

The following examples cover some common car problems.

• *Gasorin ga kireta.*

I've run out of gas.

• *Enjin ga koshō shita.*

I'm having engine trouble.

• *Kagi o ireta mama rokku shite shimatta.*

I've locked the keys inside the car.

• *Sharin ga sokkō ni ochite shimatta.*

One wheel is stuck in the ditch.

Planning a Trip

Travel agents will reserve accommodations as well as train and plane tickets. They also can book customers on inexpensive package deals.

TRAVEL AGENT:

Irasshaimase.

May I help you?

CUSTOMER:

Raigetsu Kyūshū e ryokō shitain' desu ga, tomaru tokoro o sagashite imasu.

I want to travel to Kyushu next month and I'm looking for somewhere to stay.

TRAVEL AGENT:

Nanpaku desu ka?

For how many nights?

CUSTOMER:

Ni-haku. Takakunai yado no hō ga ii no desu ga.

Two nights. A place that's not expensive would be best.

TRAVEL AGENT:

Kore wa ikaga desu ka? Ryokan desu kedo. Nishoku-tsuki desu. Mata, kō iu mono deshitara, ressha no unchin ga niwari-biki ni narimasu.

How about this? It's a Japanese inn and it comes with two meals. Or, if you choose one of these (places), you'll get a twenty percent reduction on the train fares.

CUSTOMER:

Arigatō gozaimasu. Kangaete mimasu.

Thank you. I'll think about it.

Making a Room Reservation

When you call to make reservations for a room, you should always confirm the rates. In this dialogue, the operator at a Japanese inn has just transferred the caller to the front desk.

RECEPTIONIST:

Hai, furonto desu.

This is the front desk.

CALLER:

Nijū-roku-nichi ippaku yoyaku shitain' desu ga, heya wa arimasu ka?

I'd like to make a reservation for one night, on the twenty-sixth. Do you have any rooms available?

RECEPTIONIST:

Hai. Nanmei-sama deshō ka?

OK. For how many people?

CALLER:

Otona futari ni, kodomo hitori desu. Ryōkin wa ikura ni narimasu ka?

Two adults and one child. How much will it be?

RECEPTIONIST:

Nishoku-tsuki, zeisābisu-komi de, ichiman nisen-en desu ga, o-kosama wa sono gojuppāsento ni narimasu.

With two meals, tax, and service charge included, it will be twelve thousand yen. The child is half-price.

CALLER:

Heya to chōshoku dake o-negai dekimasu ka?

Can we have just the room and breakfast?

RECEPTIONIST:

Hai. Otona wa kyūsen-en ni narimasu.

Yes. That would be nine thousand yen per adult.

CALLER:

Ja, sore o o-negai shimasu.

That'll be fine.

Canceling a Room Reservation

Unless you have paid in advance, you usually will not be charged for canceling a room reservation.

RECEPTIONIST:

Rizōto Hoteru de gozaimasu.

The Resort Hotel.

CALLER:

Hatsuka ni ippaku yoyaku shita Sumisu desu ga, kyanseru shitain' desu.

My name is Smith and I have made a reservation for one night on the twentieth. I would like, however, to cancel that reservation.

RECEPTIONIST:

Sō desu ka? Wakarimashita. Mata dōzo.

OK, that's fine. Please think of us next time.

CALLER:

Dōmo sumimasen deshita.

Thank you. (*lit.,* I'm very sorry.)

Using the In-house Telephone

If you are staying at a *ryokan, minshuku,* or *penshon,* you should arrive by about five o'clock because dinner is usually served around six. Japanese hotels and *ryokan* generally supply cotton sleeping

115

kimono, soap, razors, toothbrushes, and toothpaste. Hotels usually provide Western-style bath towels but *ryokan* do not.

Near the phone in the room, there should be a telephone guide with information like the following:

9	フロント	*furonto*	front desk
0	外線	*gaisen*	outside line
7	客室	*kyaku-shitsu*	other guest rooms
6	ルームサービス	*rūmu sābisu*	room service

If you need something, telephone either the front desk or room service.

- *Moshi-moshi. Sanbyaku-san gō-shitsu desu ga, kōri/ōkina yukata/rāmen o motte kite kudasai.*
  Hello? This is room 303. Can you bring some ice/a large cotton kimono/a bowl of noodles?
- *Ekusutora-beddo o tanondan' desu ga, heya ni haitte imasen.*
  We ordered an extra bed, but it's not in the room.
- *Ashita no asa wa yōshoku, o-negai dekimasu ka?*
  For tomorrow morning, can we have Western-style breakfasts?
- *Massāji, o-negai shimasu.*
  I'd like to have a massage, please.

The Hot Spring

Many people's idea of a good rest is a few days away from it all at a rustic hot spring. Because the different minerals in the water are recommended for various, often chronic, ailments, people used to spend several weeks at a hot spring. Especially in recent times, an overnight stay, often in a group, is more common. So that they get their money's worth, many people bathe from three to five times during an overnight stay.

Many places allow nonguests to use their bath, so if you are caught on a cold and rainy day, why not give up on sightseeing and take a soothing bath instead? For those who want to relax for a little while, rooms can also often be rented for just a couple of hours.

- *Sumimasen. Shukuhaku dewa naku o-furo dake hairemasu ka?*
  Excuse me. We're not staying the night but may we still use the bath?
- *Tomari dewa naku kyūkei shitai no desu ga, heya wa aite imasu ka?*
  We won't be staying the night but we'd like to rest for a while. Do you have any rooms available?
- *Koko no onsen wa nani ni kikimasu ka?*
  What is this hot spring good for?
- *Kono onsen wa ichō/ryūmachi/yōtsū/hifu-byō ni yoku kikimasu yo.*
  This hot spring is very good for stomach disorders/rheumatism/backache/skin diseases.
- *Chotto umete ii desu ka?*
  Do you mind if I add a bit of cold water?

117

Asking Where to Go

Near most major train stations, there will be a tourist information center. The staff there will not only tell you the area's places of interest, *meisho,* they might even make lodging reservations for you as well.

Also, the staff at your lodging should be able to suggest where to go and what to see in the area.

GUEST:

Chotto o-kiki shimasu ga, kono hen no meisho o oshiete kudasai.

May I ask you a question? Can you tell me about the places of interest around here?

RECEPTIONIST:

Hai. O-shiro ga yūmei desu yo. Saiken shita mono desu ga, naka ni subarashii hakubutsu-kan ga arimasu.

All right. The castle is famous. It's a reconstruction but there's a superb museum inside.

GUEST:

Machi ni dentō-teki na mingei-hin o utte iru mise nado wa arimasen ka?

Are there any shops in town selling traditional craft items?

RECEPTIONIST:

Chōchin no mise ga arimasu. Mata soko dewa, tsukutte iru tokoro mo misete kuremasu yo.

There's a paper-lantern shop. They'll also show you them being made.

GUEST:

Chōchin. Ii desu ne. Basho o oshiete kudasai. Sore-kara, mō hitotsu. O-hiru o taberu no wa doko ga ii deshō?

Paper lanterns. That would be nice. Can you tell me where it is? And there's one more thing. Where would be a good place to have lunch?

Reading a Travel Brochure

Look for packages giving bargains on transportation and accommodations. Many follow a busy itinerary but some, like this package deal to Kyushu, offer only transportation and accommodation.

フリープラン　九州

2泊3日／往復飛行機

旅行代金(1名様)

3名1室利用　おとな　44,800 円
　　　　　　こども　39,000 円
2名1室利用　おとな　46,800 円

宿泊　九州グランド・ホテル（洋室風呂付）
＊料金は朝食、税、サービス料などを含む

furii puran　Kyūshū

Ni-haku mikka/ōfuku hikōki

Ryokō daikin (ichimei-sama)
San-mei isshitsu riyō :　Otona　¥ 44,800
　　　　　　　　　　　Kodomo　¥ 39,000
Ni-mei isshitsu riyō :　Otona　¥ 46,800
Shukuhaku : Kyūshū Gurando Hoteru (Yōshitsu furo-tsuki)
* Ryōkin wa chōshoku, zei, sābisu-ryō nado o fukumu.

"Free plan" tour to Kyushu

Two nights-three days/round trip by airplane

Cost (per person)
3 to a room:　Adults　¥44,800
　　　　　　　Children　¥39,000
2 to a room:　Adults　¥46,800
Accommodation: Kyushu Grand Hotel (Western-style room with bath)
* The cost includes breakfast, tax, and service charges.

Public Holidays in Japan

In Japan, when a holiday falls on a Sunday, the following Monday becomes a holiday as well. This Monday is referred to as *furi-kae kyūjitsu* (*lit.*, transferred holiday).

Reservations for any holiday must be made months in advance. If you drive, consider traveling at night or setting off at dawn to avoid heavy traffic jams, especially around the New Year period (December 29 to January 4), Golden Week (April 29 to May 5), and the Bon Festival (August 13 to 16).

January 1	*Ganjitsu*	New Year's Day
January 15	*Seijin no Hi*	Coming of Age Day
February 11	*Kenkoku Kinen-bi*	National Founding Day
March 21	*Shunbun no Hi*	Spring Equinox Day
April 29	*Midori no Hi*	Greenery Day
May 3	*Kenpō Kinen-bi*	Constitution Day
May 4	*Kokumin no Kyūjitsu*	National Holiday
May 5	*Kodomo no Hi*	Children's Day
September 15	*Keirō no Hi*	Respect for the Aged Day
September 23	*Shūbun no Hi*	Autumnal Equinox
October 10	*Taiiku no Hi*	Health-Sports Day
November 3	*Bunka no Hi*	Culture Day
November 23	*Kinrō Kansha no Hi*	Labor Thanksgiving Day
December 23	*Tennō Tanjo-bi*	Emperor's Birthday

Useful Words and Expressions

ACCOMMODATIONS

shukuhaku	accommodations
hoteru	Western-style hotel
ryokan	Japanese inn
minshuku	family-run guesthouse
penshon	Western-style guesthouse
bijinesu hoteru	no-frills hotel, frequented mainly by businessmen
tomareru tera	temple offering accommodations
hoyō-jo	company-owned resort lodging
yūsu hosuteru	youth hostel

kokumin shukusha	national hostel
kyanpu-jō	campsite
ippaku	one-night stay
washitsu	Japanese-style room (with *futon*)
yōshitsu	Western-style room (with bed)
heya no kagi	room key
chōshoku	breakfast
ohiru-gohan/chūshoku	lunch
yūshoku	dinner
furonto	front desk
dai-yokujō	main communal bath
baiten	hotel shop

TRAVELING BY TRAIN

densha	electric train
kisha	steam train
ressha	train, often refers to a scheduled train
shinkansen	bullet train
yakō ressha	overnight train
jiyū-seki	unreserved seat
shitei-seki	reserved seat
kin'en-seki	nonsmoking seat
seisan-jo	fare-adjustment office
eki no deguchi	station exit
Midori no Mado-guchi	Japan Railways reservation office
jikoku-hyō	timetable

TRAVELING BY CAR

kōsoku dōro	expressway
ryōkin-jo	toll gate
rasshu-awā	rush hour
kōtsū no jūtai	traffic jam
sābisu eria	rest area
pākingu eria	rest area with limited facilities
dōro chizu	road map
renta-kā	car rental

8 Entertaining

FIRST-TIME VISITORS who are entertained by their Japanese hosts may be overwhelmed by the fast-paced drinking and the constant moving from one place to another. In Japan, businessmen often have a meal at a restaurant, move on to a series of bars and nightclubs, and end up at an all-night shop that serves coffee. This type of barhopping is known as *hashigo-zake,* which literally means saké ladder. Climbing this ladder can be fun but it can also be exhausting.

Beer, whiskey, and saké are the most popular alcoholic beverages in Japan. Traditional customs for drinking saké or beer are simple; raise your glass when it is being filled and then fill the glass of the other person. You should not pour your own drink. Some people fill to get a refill, so your glass being constantly topped to the rim may simply mean that your partner wants more to drink!

At an *enkai,* a party held in a *tatami* room, people move around pouring saké or beer for others. Although one really should go around once pouring for everyone, at large parties many people just pour for the VIPs. If you want to move from where you are sitting, it is quite all right to get a bottle, move to another person, offer a drink, and talk for a while.

A traditional Japanese meal at an established restaurant is not as hectic as an *enkai.* Generally speaking, a typical dinner starts with hors d'oeuvres and saké or beer, and continues, in order, with sashimi, tempura, and fish and/or meat dishes. Vegetable side dishes are brought out throughout the meal. Rice, *chazuke* (rice in tea), or sometimes *soba* (buckwheat noodles) mark the end of the meal and the drinking.

You should not worry that you are being rude if you turn down food; in fact, the Japanese themselves do not feel obligated to eat all that is offered. To be polite, you can comment on the food's appearance and be flattered by the number of dishes, but it is all right if you only eat what you like. Incidentally, children are taught not to touch food with their chopsticks (*hashi o tsukenai*) if they cannot eat the whole portion. Foreigners, however, may find that their plates are constantly being filled not by their own chopsticks, but by those of their friendly hosts.

Customs about who pays the bill are no different from those in most other countries. In business entertaining, whoever issued the invitation generally picks up the tab. When friends go out, the bill is usually split, although sometimes an older person will insist on paying. Private parties are often on a shared-cost basis with guests paying a set contribution made known when the invitation is given. In nearly all cases, the main guest is exempt from paying.

In traditional home entertaining, the wife was kept so busy in the kitchen that she did not eat with the guests. Nowadays, couples are more likely to entertain friends at home by having informal cook-at-the-table meals that allow the wife to join the fun. These get-togethers usually involve fewer than ten people and are limited just to friends.

If you like entertaining at home, remember that late-night dining is not common in Japan. You may find your plans for drinks, a leisurely dinner, and discussions late into the night disrupted by your Japanese guests arriving punctually, expecting their dinner within half an hour, and leaving early for the long journey home. Also, if you invite people for an afternoon snack, make sure they understand that you will be offering them only tea. Otherwise, they may arrive expecting dinner.

When you entertain, you may come up against what is known as *enryo* (reserve and hesitancy), the marks of a good guest in Japanese culture. Even though you urge them to make themselves at home, your Japanese guests may not start drinking or eating until you specifically ask them to start. In some rural districts, people have to be invited three times before they take a sip of their tea!

One more thing you might experience is guests accepting invitations and then not showing up. In Japan, work always take precedence over everything else, and for good or bad, attending nonbusiness-related parties and other such functions receives low priority.

In spite of the problems listed above, home entertaining can be a very enjoyable way to get to know your Japanese acquaintances. Not only will they appreciate being invited to spend time with you and your family, they will also enjoy sampling the cuisine of your home country.

Writing an Invitation

This invitation, appropriate for a postcard, serves adequately for informal parties.

パーティーのお知らせ

私の25回目のバースデー・パーティーを開きます。

日時　6月21日（日）
午後7:00より
場所　グリーン・ハイツ 303号

　1人1品、お料理を持ってきてください。飲み物とケーキ、それにメーン・ディッシュは準備しておきますのでおたのしみに。ぜひ、来てください。お待ちしています。

ジョン

Pātii no o-shirase

Watashi no nijū-go-kaime no bāsudē pātii o hirakimasu.

Nichiji:　*Rokugatsu nijū-ichi-nichi (Nichi)*
Gogo shichi-ji yori
Basho:　*Guriin Haitsu san-maru-san-gō*

Hitori hito-shina, o-ryōri o motte kite kudasai. Nomi-mono to kēki, sore ni mēn disshu wa junbi shite okimasu node o-tano-shimi ni. Zehi, kite kudasai. O-machi shite imasu.

Jon

Party Invitation
I'm giving a party for my twenty-fifth birthday.

Date: Sunday, June 21
From 7:00 p.m.

Place: Green Heights, Apt. #303

Each person please bring one dish of food. Drinks, the cake, and the main dish will be provided. Please come because it should be fun. Look forward to seeing you.

John

Inviting People

These phrases can be used to invite people to your home. In the first situation, a young man invites a friend to his house-warming party:

• *Atarashii apāto ni hikkoshitan' de, kondo no Doyōbi ni pātii o suru kedo, koreru kana?*
I'm having a party on Saturday because I've moved into a new apartment. Can you come?

Below, a young woman asks another girl to a birthday party:

• *Kazuko-san no tanjōbi dakara, raishū no Nichiyōbi ni uchi de pātii o suru kedo, irassharanai? O-ryōri o mochi-yori ni shimashō.*
I'm having a birthday party for Kazuko at my house next Sunday. Can you come? It'll be a potluck affair.

In the next example, a woman telephones the wife of a business acquaintance to invite the couple to dinner.

• *Jūku-nichi no Doyōbi, watashi no uchi de yūshoku o go-issho shitain' da-kedo, o-futari de irasshaimasen ka?*
We'd like you to join us for dinner here on Saturday, the nineteenth. Would you and your husband be able to come and join us?

Declining Invitations

In the following example, a man declines an invitation from a close friend:

• *Arigatō. Warui kedo, sono hi ni yotei ga arun' da yo.*
Thanks. I'm sorry but I've got something on that day.

A politer way to say the same thing is:

• *Artgatō gozaimasu. Zannen desu ga, sono hi ni chotto yotei ga arimashite, mōshi-wake arimasen.*
Thank you. Unfortunately I have something to do that day. I'm sorry.

This example shows how you can refuse an invitation you have already accepted:

• *Ashita no o-yakusoku no koto desu keredomo. Jitsu wa kyū na yōji ga dekimashite, shusseki dekinaku narimashita. Hontō ni zannen desu ga.*
It's about (our plans) tomorrow. Something urgent has cropped up and I won't be able to go. I'm very sorry.

Receiving Guests

You will need a clear policy on shoes because your Japanese guests may not know what is expected of them. If you wear shoes

in your home, tell guests to treat your house like a hotel. If you have a shoes-off policy, put a couple of shoes conspicuously in the entranceway and line up house slippers before the guests arrive.

These phrases will help you make the visit go smoothly.

• *O-machi shite imashita. Dōzo.*

We've been expecting you. Please come in.

• *Dōzo, o-agari kudasai.*

Please come in. (*lit.,* Please come up.)

• *Irasshai!*

Welcome! (used especially for unexpected guests)

• *Kutsu no mama, dōzo.*

Please keep your shoes on.

• *Dōzo kochira e.*

Please come this way.

• *Chotto o-machi kudasai. Kōhii o motte kimasu kara.*

Just a moment. I'll get some coffee.

• *O-cha, dōzo.*

Please have some tea./Please go ahead and drink your tea.

• *Jibun de tsukutte mitan' desu keredo, yoroshikattara kukkii, dōzo.*

Please try a cookie. I made them myself.

• *Dōzo, tabako wa go-enryo kudasai. Arerugii taishitsu desu kara.*

Please don't smoke because I'll get an allergic reaction to it.

• *Michi wa sugu wakarimashita ka?*

Did you easily find your way?

Visiting Someone's Home

When you reach your destination, ring the doorbell and announce your name through the interphone. If there is no doorbell, open the door and announce your arrival with *Gomen kudasai.*

How should you leave your shoes in the entranceway? Strictly speaking, you should leave your shoes facing toward the inside of the house, and at some point during your stay they will most likely be turned around to face the outside, ready for leaving.

This custom stems from the fact that it is apparently bad form to back up into a house. Nowadays, women usually turn their shoes around when entering, and children are trained to do the same. One rarely, however, sees grown men turn their shoes.

When you visit someone's home, you will find these phrases useful to know:

- *Shitsurei shimasu./O-jama shimasu.*
  Excuse me. (say this when you take your shoes off and again when you enter the living room)
- *Dōzo, o-kamai naku.*
  Please don't go to any trouble. (if offered tea or drinks)
- *O-isogashii tokoro, arigatō gozaimashita.*
  Thank you for making time to see us.
- *O-sake wa itadakenai mono desukara, yoroshikattara o-mizu o itadake-masen ka?*
  I don't drink alcohol. Could I have some water instead?
- *Tabako o sutte mo ii desu ka?*
  May I smoke?
- *Sumimasen. O-tearai o o-kari shitain' desu ga.*
  May I use the bathroom?
- *Ii o-sumai desu ne.*
  What a nice place you have.
- *Suteki na chawan desu ne. Hagi deshō ka?*
  What a beautiful teacup! Is it *Hagi* pottery?
- *O-kosama, irasshaimasu ka?*
  Do you have any children?
- *O-kosama, nannin irasshaimasu ka?*
  How many children do you have?

Introducing Guests

This dialogue shows how you can introduce someone at a reception.
HOST:

O-hanashi no tochū de sumimasen. Zehi go-shōkai shitai kata ga imasu. Inagaki Kyōju, kochira wa Monbu-shō no gakusei no Janetto Chen-san desu.

I'm sorry to interrupt. There is someone I'd very much like

you to meet. Professor Inagaki, this is Miss Janet Chen, a Ministry of Education student.

GUEST:

Hon Kon Daigaku no Chen desu. Hajimemashite.

My name is Chen and I'm from Hong Kong University. I'm pleased to meet you.

PROFESSOR INAGAKI:

Inagaki desu. Dōzo yoroshiku.

My name is Inagaki. I'm glad to meet you.

Commenting on the Food

In this dialogue, a couple has been invited to dinner at the home of a Japanese acquaintance. The wife is delighted by the beautiful presentation but her husband is dubious about the food.

HOSTESS:

O-shokuji ga dekimashita node, dōzo. * * * *Nani-mo gozaimasen ga, dōzo meshi-agatte kudasai.*

Dinner is ready. * * * I hope you like it. (*lit.,* There is nothing.) Please go ahead and start.

EVERYONE:

Itadakimasu.

Bon appetit. (*lit.,* I receive.)

HOSTESS:

Dōzo, o-tori kudasai. Nihon ryōri wa o-kuchi ni aimasu ka?

Please help yourself. Do you like Japanese food?

WIFE:

Ē. Sappari shite oishii desu ne.

Yes, it's light and very delicious.

HOSTESS:

Biru-san wa?

How about you, Bill?

HUSBAND:

Boku ni wa chotto narenai aji desu ne.

I'm not really used to the taste.

WIFE:

Zenbu wa kirei desu ne. Mori-tsuke mo hitotsu-hitotsu betsu nan desu ne.

131

Utsuwa mo suteki desu. Demo, osara-arai ga taihen deshō.
It's all beautiful. It's all arranged in different dishes. The
tableware is lovely too. But it must be a lot of washing up.

HOSTESS:

Sō demo nain' desu. Mō sukoshi ikaga desu ka?
Not really. How about a little more?

WIFE:

Kekkō desu. Takusan itadakimashita.
No more, thank you. I've had a lot to eat.

Taking Clients Out to Dinner

When you entertain Japanese clients, you may prefer to take them
to a restaurant serving Western-style cuisine. That way, you can
maintain your role as the host when it comes to ordering.

HOST:

Nani o tabemashō ka? Koko no shefu no o-susume ryōri wa oishii desu yo.
What shall we have? The chef's special menu is good.

CLIENT:

Sakana kōsu ni shimasu.
I'll have the fish dinner.

HOST: (to waiter)

O-negai shimasu! Sakana kōsu hitotsu ni sutēki kōsu hitotsu o-negai shimasu.
Waiter! One fish dinner and one steak dinner, please.

WAITER:

Hai. Kashikomarimashita.
Yes, sir.

HOST: (to client)

Wain, ikaga desu ka?
How about some wine?

CLIENT:

Ii desu ne. Itadakimashō.
Fine. Let's have some.

HOST:

Nani-ka suki na wain, arimasu ka?
Do you have any preferences in wine?

CLIENT:
   Wain nara, o-makase shimasu.
   I'll leave the wine up to you.
HOST: (to waiter)
   Kono Bōjorē o ippon kudasai.
   One bottle of this Beaujolais, please.

Making Small Talk

The following phrases are suitable for small talk at receptions and parties. If you want to excuse yourself, bow slightly and say to the person you are talking to, *Chotto shitsurei shimasu* (Excuse me).

- *Dochira no go-shusshin desu ka?*
  Where were you born?
- *Mō Amerika wa nagain' desu ka?*
  Have you been in the United States long?
- *O-shigoto wa?*
  What's your job?
- *O-sumai wa dochira desu ka?*
  Where do you live?
- *Kanada e irasshatta koto ga arimasu ka?*
  Have you ever been to Canada?
- *Ano, o-kao wa yoku zonji-agete orimasu ga, o-namae no hō ga dete konakute . . . * * * A, sō deshita! Shitsurei shimashita. Nihongo no namae ga muzukashikute . . .*
  I know your face, but your name escapes me . . . * * * That's right! I'm sorry. Japanese names are so difficult.
- *Nani-ka tsumamimashō ka?*
  Shall we get something to eat?

Saying It's Time to Go

When it is time to go, look at your watch and say *Mō, soro-soro* (It's about time to go), a phrase that will immediately make it apparent that you have to leave. Out of politeness, your host will probably try at least once to detain you.

GUEST:

Dōmo, o-jama shimashita. Taihen gochisō ni narimashita.

Thank you for having me over. (*lit.,* I'm sorry to have bothered you.) And thank you for the meal.

HOST:

Mada iin' ja nain' desu ka?

Can't you stay longer?

GUEST:

Ashita hayai mono desukara.

I have to be up early tomorrow morning.

HOST:

Sō desu ka. Sore-dewa zehi, mata o-dekake kudasai.

I see. Then please come again.

These phrases can also be used when you leave:

• *Osoku made, o-jama shite wa mōshi-wake arimasen kara.*

I don't want to keep you up late.

• *Sono-uchi, mata yukkuri o-jama shimasu.*

I'll stay longer next time I come.

• *Dōzo kondo wa uchi ni oide kudasai.*

Come and visit us next time.

• *O-saki ni shitsurei shimasu.*

Excuse me but I've got to go. (said to other guests)

Useful Words and Expressions

mote-nashi	hospitality
settai	entertaining (usually business)
settai suru	to entertain
shōtai suru	to invite
shōtai-jō	invitation card
tsuki-ai	association, acquaintance, friendship
resepushon	reception
enkai	party, usually in a *tatami* room
risshoku pātii	buffet party
hōmu pātii	party held at home
ryōtei	traditional Japanese restaurant

zashiki	*tatami* room used for parties
niji-kai	party held immediately after another party
o-aiso	bill in sushi bars and Japanese restaurants
o-kanjō	bill in ordinary restaurants
kaihi	set contribution to a party
kaihi-sei	shared-cost basis
ogoru	to treat someone
shokuji o ogoru	to treat someone to a meal
karaoke	singing to taped accompanying music
gozen-sama	person who comes home after midnight

9 Children

Isabella Bird, a Yorkshirewoman traveling in northern Japan in 1878, observed that she had never seen "people take so much delight in their offspring, carrying them about. . . supplying them constantly with new toys, taking them to picnics and festivals."[1] Over a hundred years later, the feelings of this writer, another Yorkshirewoman, are strikingly similar. Japanese parents do not seem to resent that their children stay up late, disregard the word "no," and demand full attention day and night. In fact, Japanese mothers and fathers sometimes appear to enjoy spoiling their children.

To Westerners, Japanese parents seem indulgent, and to Japanese, Western parents seem strict. The Western parent teaches children to recognize social situations and to behave appropriately; having set down the rules, the parent usually does not tolerate children who disobey. On the other hand, the Japanese parent trains not by principle but by example. The child may not obey at first, but the mother knows that he or she eventually will.

Almost all Japanese children attend kindergarten for one, two, or three years before starting grade school. A Japanese kindergarten can teach your child Japanese, provide Japanese friends for both of you, and give you a unique opportunity to see Japanese society from the inside. You may, of course, have to resolve unexpected problems. For example, because Japanese schools often expect mothers to help out in various ways, you might not have as much free time as you anticipated. Also, you might have to conform with what other Japanese parents are doing; for instance, because all the other parents are stuffing their children's rucksacks with candy, you reluctantly may decide to allow your child to take sweets to school outings. Furthermore, you will probably have to come to terms with the emphasis on group activity. If you have difficulty accepting the values of Japanese society, you should think twice before enrolling your child in a Japanese school.

Because Japanese parents' expectations of their children are high, a large percentage of children commute to *juku,* private tutoring schools offering classes after regular school hours and on weekends. Many foreign parents have found that a *juku* can be a good place for their children not only to learn to read and write

Japanese, but also to improve in other areas like arithmetic. Also, foreign children can take advantage of the availability of instruction in a variety of non-academic fields. Virtually every neighborhood has teachers of piano, English, and abacus, and not far away there will surely be facilities for judo, kendo, ballet, violin, swimming, gymnastics, and many other activities. Fees are generally reasonable but they can mount up if you have several children taking two or three courses.

Compulsory education in Japan is for nine years; six years of elementary school followed by three years of junior high. All elementary and junior high schools throughout the country follow a standard curriculum set down by the Ministry of Education. According to Ministry of Education figures for 1987, 94.2 percent of all children go on to high school and 30 percent go on to college.

When Japanese children reach the age of ten or eleven, they become increasingly involved with school-related activities. In junior high, students stay on after school to attend semicompulsory clubs that can keep them out of the house for up to twelve hours a day, six days a week. Teenagers often go to school on Sundays for interschool matches and sometimes even for tests.

In Japan, much importance is placed on passing entrance exams. This is partly because there is a direct correlation in Japan between good universities and good work opportunities; i.e., graduating from a top-ranked university almost guarantees a job with a top-ranked company. Therefore, the whole education system is geared to preparing the student to take these university entrance exams. Entrance exams are not limited to universities only; besides exams for entering high school, exams for entering junior high schools and even grade schools recently have become commonplace.

Entrance exams are taken at age twelve for a private junior high school, at age fifteen for a private or public high school, and at age eighteen for university. Prior to exams, family members go out of their way to give the student the best conditions for studying. Summer vacations may be forgone and Christmas and New Year celebrations abbreviated all because someone is taking full-time courses to prepare for these exams. As the February exam season approaches, mothers pamper children taking exams by serving them warming snacks to tide them through the late-night cramming, and TV programs give advice on how to avoid colds that could jeopardize this chance of a lifetime. Entrance into university marks the culmination of a long, intense scholastic endeavor and college days tend to be a happy, carefree hiatus before the hardships of the working life begins.

1. Isabella Bird, *Unbeaten Tracks in Japan* (Tokyo: Tuttle, 1973), 75.

Learning a Few Basic Words

The rough and tumble of children's play knows no language barrier, but teaching these basic words to your toddler can help ease his or her way into Japanese infant society.

• *Irete.*/*Mazete.*	Can I join in?
• *Kashite.*	Can I borrow this?
• *Arigatō.*	Thanks.
• *Dame.*	No, you can't.
• *Gomen-nasai.*	Sorry.
• *Zurui.*/*Ijiwaru.*	Not fair.

These phrases are for parents:

• *O-namae wa?*	What's your name?
• *Ikutsu?*	How old are you?
• *Orikō-san.*	That's a good boy/girl.

Admiring a Baby

In this dialogue, a woman admires the baby on a neighbor's back. The infant's round face and narrow eyes peep out from under the special overcoat that keeps both the mother and child warm.

WOMAN:

Kawaii desu ne. Ōkiku narimashita ne. Ima nankagetsu?

Isn't she cute! She really has grown, hasn't she? How old is she now?

NEIGHBOR:

Jukkagetsu desu.

Ten months.

WOMAN:

Sō. Otōsan ni nite imasu ne.

Really? Doesn't she look like her father!

NEIGHBOR:

Ē, minna ni iwarerun' desu.

Yes, everyone says so.

WOMAN:

Rinyū-shoku wa? [Table food]

How's the weaning going? [Bonyū] [Breast feeding]

NEIGHBOR:

Gohan, o-tōfu, o-sakana o takusan tabete, kuda-mono mo daisuki desu.

She eats a lot of rice, tofu, and fish, and she loves fruit.

WOMAN:

Yokatta desu ne.

That's good.

NEIGHBOR:

Amerika-jin wa soi-ne o shinai'tte hontō? [sleep w/ baby] [desu ka?]

Is it true that American women don't sleep with their babies?

WOMAN:

Ē. Betsu na heya de nerun' desu.

Yes. Babies sleep in separate rooms.

NEIGHBOR:

Nihon no baai wa o-furo ni issho ni hairi, dakinagara shokuji o tabesasemasu. Dekakeru toki wa onbu o shimasu. Sukinshippu wa ii to iu kedo, ka-hogo ka-shira? [desho ka seouimasu.]

In Japan, mothers [over protect] bathe together with their babies and sit them on their laps to feed them. When they go out they put their babies on their backs. They say that "skinship" is a good thing but maybe it's being overly protective.

WOMAN:

Dō deshō ne. Shikashi, oya no nayami ga chigatte mo, dono kuni demo ikuji wa taihen desu ne. [Kahogo]

[raising ch.]

141

Perhaps. But one thing is for sure. Parents may have different problems but raising children is difficult in any country.

Asking About a Kindergarten

Some kindergartens are run by local authorities, but the majority are privately owned. Most do not give formal training in reading and arithmetic.

In this dialogue, a mother asks a neighbor about the age requirements for a neighborhood kindergarten.

PARENT:

Megumi-chan wa doko no yōchi-en e itte imasu ka?

Which kindergarten does Megumi go to?

NEIGHBOR:

Akebono Yōchi-en. Jinja no yōchi-en desu.

Akebono Kindergarten. It's run by a Shinto shrine.

PARENT:

Uchi no Erena wa hairemasu ka?

Could our Elena go there?

NEIGHBOR:

O-tanjōbi wa itsu desu ka?

When's her birthday?

PARENT:

Jūnigatsu ni yon-sai ni narimasu.
She'll be four in December.

NEIGHBOR:

Sore-dewa, rainen no Shigatsu kara ni-nen hoiku ni narimasu ne.
Then she'll start next April and go for two years.

PARENT:

Ima kara hairenain' desu ka?
Can't she start now?

NEIGHBOR:

Shigatsu ni minna issho ni nyūgaku suru no ga futsū desu ga, san-nen hoiku mo arimasu kara kiite mitara dō desu ka? Ima, Megumi o mukae ni ikimasu kara issho ni itte mimasu ka?
Usually children all start together in April but the school does take children for three years. Why don't you ask? I'm going to meet Megumi now so why don't you come along?

PARENT:

Hai. Arigatō gozaimasu.
OK. Thank you.

Introducing Yourself

If you have children attending a Japanese school, you may be asked to introduce yourself at class meetings. You can use the following, conventionally modest introduction:

Emirii Shumitto no haha desu. Sengetsu Doitsu kara mairimashita. Kodomo wa mada Nihongo o yoku hanasemasen shi, narenai koto ga ōi to omoimasu ga, yoroshiku o-negai shimasu.

I am Emily Schmidt's mother. We came from Germany last month. Emily still does not speak Japanese well and I think there are lots of things she hasn't gotten used to yet. I would appreciate it if you would look after her.

Telephoning the School

In this dialogue, a father telephones the school to inform them that his child is sick and will be absent from class.

143

TEACHER:

Hai. Akebono Yōchi-en desu.

Hello. Akebono Kindergarten.

FATHER:

Kiku gumi no Erena Mitcheru no chichi desu.

This is Eleanor Mitchell's father. Eleanor's in the "chrysanthemum" class.

TEACHER:

Hai.

Yes.

FATHER:

Kodomo ga netsu o dashimashita node, kyō wa yasumasetai to omoimasu.

Emily's got a temperature so I'd like to keep her out of school today.

TEACHER:

Wakarimashita. O-daiji ni.

I see. I hope she feels better.

FATHER:

Yoroshiku o-negai shimasu. Gomen kudasai.

Thank you. Goodbye.

Writing an Absence Note

If you go away for the weekend, you'll have to send a note informing the school that your child will be absent on Saturday morning.

Ashita (Doyōbi) kazoku de dekakeru node, Erena o yasumasete kudasai.

Because the family is going out of town, please excuse Eleanor from school tomorrow (Saturday).

Inviting Children to a Party

A good way to get to know the neighbors is to invite their children to a party. When talking to other parents, use the honorific verb *irassharu* when referring to their children.

MOTHER:

Nijū-ni-nichi ni Kurisumasu pātii o uchi de shimasu ga, Satomi-chan to Kenta-kun, irasshaimasen ka? Ato de kādo o kodomo ni motasemasu.

We're having a Christmas party on the twenty-second. Can Satomi and Kenta come? I'll send the children round later with an invitation.

NEIGHBOR:

Arigatō gozaimasu.

Thank you.

MOTHER:

Shimizu-san to Mori-san no kodomo-san mo kimasu ga, yoroshikattara dōzo.

The Shimizu and Mori children are coming, so I hope your children can come as well.

NEIGHBOR:

Hai. Dōmo arigatō gozaimasu. Kodomo ga kitto yorokobu deshō.

Thank you very much. The children will be delighted.

MOTHER:

Zehi, dōzo. O-machi shite orimasu.

Please come. We look forward to seeing them.

Visiting the Pediatrician

You can take a sick child to a neighborhood pediatrician or to the pediatric ward of a general hospital. You probably will have to show your insurance card or settle the method of payment before treatment is given.

DOCTOR:

Dō shimashita ka?

What's the matter?

PARENT:

Kinō no yoru kara netsu o dashimashita.

She's had a fever since last night.

DOCTOR:

Kinō nan-do deshita ka?

What was her temperature yesterday?

PARENT:

Sanjū-hachi-do nana-bu arimashita.

It was 38.7 degrees centigrade.

145

DOCTOR:
Geri wa?
Any diarrhea?

PARENT:
Geri wa shite imasen.
No, no diarrhea.

DOCTOR:
Hakimashita ka?
Did she vomit?

PARENT:
Iie. Hakimasen deshita.
No, no vomiting.

DOCTOR:
*Dewa chotto shinsatsu shimasu ne. * * * Taishita koto nai to omoimasu. Suibun o takusan ataete kudasai. Kaze-gusuri to genetsu-zai o dashimasu.*

I'll go ahead and examine her. * * * I don't think it's anything serious. Give her lots of fluids. I'll give her some medicine for the cold and something to bring the fever down.

PARENT:
Arigatō gozaimashita.
Thank you very much.

Describing Ailments

You might need to use one of the following phrases to help the doctor understand what is wrong with your child.

• *Nodo ga itai.*
  He has a sore throat.
• *Karada ga darui.*
  He feels listless.
• *Piinattsu ga nodo ni tsumatte iru.*
  He's got a peanut stuck in his throat.
• *Kaidan kara ochite, te o kitte, atama o utta.*
  He fell down the stairs, cut his hand, and hit his head.
• *Kizetsu shita.*
  He fainted.

- *Hossa o okoshita.*
  He's had a spasm.
- *Ishiki-fumei ni natta.*
  He became unconscious.

Asking About Swimming Lessons

Many swimming pools offer courses both for adults and for children. In this dialogue, a mother asks about swimming lessons for babies.

PARENT:

Uchi no kodomo ni suiei o sasetain' desu ga, koko wa bebii suimingu wa arimasu ka?

I'd like my child to take swimming lessons. Do you have classes for babies here?

SWIMMING COACH:

Hai, dekimasu. Kōsu wa Getsuyōbi to Mokuyōbi no jū-ji-han kara jū-ichi-ji made desu.

Yes, we do. The course is on Mondays and Thursdays from 10:30 to 11:00.

PARENT:

Nankagetsu kara dekimasu ka?

From what age can babies start?

SWIMMING COACH:

Sankagetsu kara desu.

From three months.

PARENT:

Gessha wa ikura desu ka?

How much are the lessons per month?

SWIMMING COACH:

Nyūkai-kin wa yonsen-en, gessha wa gosen-en desu.

There's an entrance fee of four thousand yen and then a monthly fee of five thousand yen.

PARENT:

Mizu wa tsumetakunain' desu ka?

Is the water cold?

SWIMMING COACH:

Akachan sen'yō no pūru ga gozaimashite, suion ga itsumo sanjū-ni-do ijō ni natte orimasu. Go-annai shimashō ka?

There's a baby pool where the water is always over 32°. Shall I show you around?

PARENT:

Hai. O-negai shimasu.

Yes, please.

Meeting Your Child's Teacher

If you notice something wrong with your child's behavior, you can discuss the problem with his or her teacher. You can usually find teachers working in the staff room until the evening.

PARENT:

Gomen kudasai. Koizumi Sensei, o-negai shimasu.

Excuse me. I'd like to see Mr. Koizumi.

SCHOOL OFFICIAL:

Hai. Shōshō o-machi kudasai.

Yes. Please wait one moment.

PARENT: (As teacher approaches)

Itsumo o-sewa ni narimasu. Chotto go-sōdan shitai koto ga arimashite. . .

We're much obliged to you. Could I have a word with you?

TEACHER:

*Hai. Kyōshitsu e ikimashō.   * * *   Dewa, dōzo o-hanashi kudasai.*

OK. Let's go to the classroom.   * * *   Well, what would you like to discuss?

PARENT:

Jon ga konogoro shizunde ite, yōsu ga itsumo to chigau mono desukara, ki ni narimashite . . .

John is depressed these days. He's not the same as usual, so I've been worried.

TEACHER:

Sō desu ka? Kyōshitsu dewa akarukute, benkyō ni hagende imasu. Seiseki mo ii hō da shi, shinpai wa iranai to omoimasu keredomo. Tomodachi to yoku asonde imasu ka?

Is that so? He's cheerful in class and works hard. His marks are above average so I don't think there's need for concern. Does he play with his friends a lot?

PARENT:

Iie. Hitori de famikon de asonde imasu.

No. He plays TV games by himself.

TEACHER:

Ja, tomodachi dōshi de nani-ka ga atta no kamo-shiremasen ne. Ashita kiite mimashō.

Then he may have had some trouble with his friends. I'll try and find out tomorrow.

PARENT:

Arigatō gozaimasu.

Thank you very much.

TEACHER:

Denwa demo ii desukara, mata nani-ka attara renraku shite kudasai.

If there's anything else I can do, please get in touch. It's all right to phone.

Useful Words and Expressions

BIRTH

Omedeta desu ka?	Are you expecting?
ninshin suru	to be pregnant
sankyū	maternity leave
sanfujin-ka	obstetrics and gynecology
o-san	birth, delivery
bunben-shitsu	delivery room
o-san ni tachi-au	to be present at the birth

BABIES

bonyū	breast-feeding
miruku	formula, milk preparation
honyū-bin	feeding bottle
oppai o yaru	to breastfeed a baby
oppai o nomu	to drink from the breast
rinyū-shoku	baby food
kami o-mutsu	disposable diapers
onbu o suru	to carry on the back
dakko o suru	to carry in the arms
bagii	stroller
bebii-beddo	crib
komori-uta	lullaby

CHILDHOOD ILLNESSES AND MEDICAL TERMS

hentō-sen	tonsillitis
ryūkan/infuruenza	influenza
chūji-en	middle ear infection
hashika	measles
mizu-bōsō	chicken pox
otafuku-kaze	mumps
fūshin	German measles
shōni zensoku	infantile asthma
atopi	atopic dermatitus
Nihon nōen	Japanese encephalitis
porio/shōni mahi	polio
hyakunichi-zeki	whooping cough
jifuteria	diptheria
hashōfu	tetanus
kossetsu	fracture
kenkō shindan	medical checkup
yobō sesshu	vaccination
sanshu kongō	triple vaccination (tetanus, whooping cough, and diptheria)

SCHOOL

hoiku-en	nursery school
yōchi-en	kindergarten
shō-gakkō	elementary school

chū-gakkō	junior high
kōtō gakkō/kōkō	high school
juku	private tutoring school offering classes after regular school hours
nyūgaku shiken	school entrance exams
juken	taking entrance exams
suberi-dome	back-up choice of school, especially university, when taking entrance exams
nyūgaku-shiki	entrance ceremony
sotsugyō-shiki	graduation ceremony
tōkō suru	to go to school
tōkō kyohi	refusing to go to school
randoseru	knapsack
undō-kai	sports day; field day
ensoku	school outing
kumi	class
san-nen ichi-kumi	class one of third grade
sensei	teacher
jugyō	lesson
sankan-bi	school observation day
seiseki-hyō/tsūshin-bo	report card
bukatsu	club activities
hōka-go	after-school hours
o-keiko/narai-goto	lessons (in piano, judo, etc.)
gakkō o yasumu	to be absent from school
ijime	bullying
kōkō chūtai	dropping out of high school
kōnai bōryoku	school violence

10   Officialdom

FOREIGNERS as well as the Japanese often complain about how hard it sometimes is to deal with governmental officials. The inefficiency and lack of courtesy that characterize governmental offices sharply contrast with the tremendous vitality and excellent service found in the private sector. Simple procedures such as renewing a work visa require that you appear in person at an immigration office, fill in a great deal of paperwork, and wait for hours to get processed. Getting mad and demanding action, a ploy that works in many parts of the world, may not be effective in Japan. Rather, officials are often impressed by foreigners who politely cooperate without making a fuss. Being submissive is often the quickest way to get what you want.

If you come to Japan to live for a while, you probably need to get an alien registration card. Take your passport and two passport photographs to the the ward or city office and, after being fingerprinted, you will receive either a card or a plastic certificate. The card usually is valid for five years and should be carried at all times. There is a movement against being fingerprinted, but so far legal cases have met with little success. If you refuse to be fingerprinted, you may end up in court.

During your stay in Japan, you might be asked to produce a document showing proof of residence. This document, called the *tōroku-zumi shōmei-sho,* is obtained from the same section at the city or ward office that handles alien registration. Also, if you marry a Japanese, you must go and register at the city or ward office. Copies of this registration document, the *koseki,* are required as proof of identity for all sorts of procedures like applying for licenses and enrolling in schools. Depending on the situation, you will need either the *tōhon,* which is a copy of the register for the whole family, or the *shōhon,* which is a copy of the register just for an individual.

Other occasions requiring a visit to the city or ward office are births, deaths, and changes of address. The staff there will also help you with matters like health insurance, pensions, and welfare.

If you use a name seal instead of a signature for legal documents, this seal, called *jitsu-in,* should be registered at the city or ward office. A certificate of registration issued within the past three months has to be produced every time the seal is used. Even if you decide not to use a name seal, your signature on legal documents has to be notorized by a certificate, called *sain shōmei-sho*, which can be obtained from the embassy. A name seal used at a bank, the *todoke-in*, does not have to be registered, but make sure you use the same seal for all transactions done at that one bank. Finally, any seal, a *mitome-in*, can be used for such mundane tasks as receiving parcels. Name seals should be looked after with the utmost care and should never be loaned to anyone; people have had their homes signed away as collateral for fraudulent loans.

Your most serious bouts with Japanese officialdom will probably be with the personnel at Immigration. Because your stay in Japan depends upon their approval, you cannot avoid the time-consuming chore of going to Immigration and having your visa renewed. One possible tactic is to treat this task like an obstacle course against the clock. Learn the system, aim for efficiency, and try to beat your best time. Telephone beforehand to find out what documents you need. When you arrive, ask for the appropriate forms, fill them in, and immediately line up to be processed.

If your visa has expired, go immediately to Immigration and apologize. Keep in mind that if you are apprehended after your visa has expired, you can be deported. Remember too that you need a re-entry permit from Immigration if you temporarily leave the country. If you frequently travel abroad, you should consider getting a multiple re-entry permit, which allows you to leave and return an unlimited number of times within a certain time period.

Finally, what should you know about driving a car in Japan? First, when you buy a car, you need your alien registration card and a document verifying that you have a parking space. This document, the *shako shōmei-sho*, can be obtained from the police. As for obtaining a Japanese driver's license, simply take your foreign license to the licensing center for your area and fill in the appropriate forms. The procedure itself is easy, but it can take time to get processed. When you drive, keep to the frustratingly low speed limits and be careful that you do not park illegally. And

155

lastly, never drink and drive; instead, take a taxi or call one of the driving services (*daikō*) to drive both you and your car to your home.

Extending Your Visa

Before you go to Immigration to extend your visa, you should telephone to find out what documents you need.

OFFICIAL:

Nyūkoku Kanri Jimu-sho.

Immigration Office.

FOREIGNER:

Moshi-moshi. Ei-kaiwa no kyōshi o shite iru Amerika-jin desu ga, biza no kōshin ni dō iu shorui ga hitsuyō desu ka?

Hello. I'm an American teacher of English. What documents do I need to renew my visa?

OFFICIAL:

Gakkō ga hoshō-nin to natte irun' desu ka?

Is the school your sponsor?

FOREIGNER:

Sō desu. Gakkō no riji-chō desu.

Yes. The director of the school.

OFFICIAL:

Soredewa desu ne, riji-chō ga kaita hoshō-sho to gensen chōshū shōmei-sho, soshite keiyaku-sho, sorekara anata no gaikoku-jin tōroku shōmei-sho to pasupōto o motte kite kudasai.

Then you will need a letter of guarantee from the director, his certificate of tax withheld, and your work contract. Also, please bring your alien registration card and passport.

FOREIGNER:

Hai. Arigatō gozaimashita.

I see. Thank you.

Forgetting to Renew Your Visa

If you have committed this cardinal sin, go straight to Immigration and apologize.

FOREIGNER:

Sumimasen. Zairyū kyoka no kōshin o wasurete shimattan' desu ga.

Excuse me. I've forgotten to extend my visa.

OFFICIAL:

Ē! Itsu kireta?

What! When did it expire?

FOREIGNER:

Sengetsu no nijū-go-nichi desu.

The twenty-fifth of last month.

OFFICIAL:

Naze konakatta no? Kireta mama da to taiho sareta kamo-shiremasen yo.

Why didn't you come? With an expired visa you could have been arrested.

FOREIGNER:

Mōshi-wake arimasen. Ukkari shite shimaimashita. Hontō ni sumimasen deshita.

I'm very sorry. It just slipped my mind. I'm truly sorry.

OFFICIAL:

Ki ga tsuite sassoku koko ni kita kara, mada yokatta desu yo. Soredewa, kono shorui o kaite kudasai.

It's a good thing you came here as soon as you realized. Well, fill in these forms, please.

FOREIGNER:

Hai. Dōmo arigatō gozaimashita.

All right. Thank you very much.

Obtaining a Re-entry Permit

Most foreigners get their re-entry permits the same time that they get or renew their work visas. The procedure is simple and is usually not time-consuming.

In this dialogue, an airport official discovers that a foreigner going abroad has forgotten to get a re-entry permit.

OFFICIAL:

Sai-nyūkoku kyoka-sho ga kono pasupōto ni wa arimasen yo!

There's no re-entry permit in this passport!

157

TRAVELER:

A, wasurete shimaimashita!

Oh, no! I forgot!

OFFICIAL: (leading the traveler to the airport immigration office)

Chotto kochira e dōzo. Nihon o deru no wa hajimete ja nai deshō?

Come this way, please. This is not the first time you've left Japan, is it?

TRAVELER:

Ē. Sō desu.

No, it isn't. (*lit.*, Yes, that's correct.)

OFFICIAL:

Naze kyoka o toranakattan' desu ka?

Why didn't you get a permit?

TRAVELER:

Shigoto ga isogashikute, sono ue ryokō no junbi de, sukkari wasurete shimaimashita.

I was so busy at work and at getting ready for the trip that I completely forgot.

OFFICIAL:

Mata Nihon ni kaette kuru tsumori deshō?

You plan on coming back to Japan, don't you?

TRAVELER:

Ē.

Yes.

OFFICIAL:

Sai-nyūkoku kyoka ga nai to, saisho kara suteppu o funde, ima no sannen no biza ga moraerun' desu. Sai-nyūkoku kyoka o wasureru to, ato de anata ga taihen desu yo.

Without a re-entry permit, you'll have to start from step one and work back up to your three-year visa. If you forget your re-entry permit, it's tough on you later on.

TRAVELER:

Sō desu ne. Kono baai dō shitara ii deshō ka?

I see. What should I do now?

OFFICIAL:

Konkai ni kagiri koko de oshite agemasu.

Just this time, I'll stamp (your passport) here.

TRAVELER:

Yokatta. Tasukarimashita. Arigatō.

Thank goodness. That's a great help. Thank you.

OFFICIAL:

Kore-kara wasurenaide kudasai.

Please don't forget again.

TRAVELER:

Hai. Arigatō gozaimashita.

No, I won't. Thank you very much.

Losing Your Registration Card

If you happen to accidentally lose your alien registration card, you are required to contact your city or ward office within fourteen days.

FOREIGNER:

Sumimasen ga, watashi wa gaijin tōroku-sho o nakushite shimaimashita.

Excuse me, but I've lost my alien registration card.

OFFICIAL:

Itsu desu ka?

When did you lose it?

FOREIGNER:

Ototoi. Saifu goto nusumaremashita.

The day before yesterday, I had my purse and everything in it stolen.

OFFICIAL:

Shashin to pasupōto o motte kimashita ka?

Have you brought photographs and your passport?

FOREIGNER:

Hai. Shashin ni-mai desu ne.

Yes. Two photographs.

OFFICIAL:

Sore-dewa, koko ni namae, jūsho, nakushita hi to jōkyō o kaite kudasai.

OK. Then please write your name, address, and when and how you lost it here.

Getting Stopped for Speeding

If you are pulled over for speeding, should you pretend that you do not speak a single word of Japanese? Be warned. Some policemen speak good English. If you know you are in the wrong, it is probably wise to apologize and to bow as best you can from behind the steering wheel!

POLICEMAN:

Menkyo-shō o misete kudasai. Gaikoku-jin tōroku shōmei-sho mo dōzo. Sakki rokujū-san-kiro dashite imashita ne.

Show me your driver's license, please. And your alien registration card. You were doing sixty-three kilometers per hour just now.

DRIVER:

Sō desu ka? Tsui.

Was I? I didn't realize.

POLICEMAN: (looking at license)

O-namae to go-jūsho wa kore de ii desu ne.

The name and address on this are correct, aren't they?

DRIVER:

Hai.

Yes.

POLICEMAN:

Yōshi ga todokimasu node, bakkin o harai-konde kudasai. Ihan tensū wa ni-ten ni narimasu. Sankagetsu inai ni ihan ga nakereba, shizen ni kiemasu kara. Kore-kara ki o tsukete kudasai.

We will send you a form for paying the fine. You will be given two points for the offense, but if you have no offenses in the next three months, the points will be taken off. Please be careful from now on.

Traffic Violations

In Japan, driving offenses are tallied by points. A total of six points leads to a suspension of between 30 and 180 days, and fifteen points leads to disqualification, which involves retaking the driving test. There are stiffer penalties for frequent offenders.

On the other hand, if you have had a clean record for the last two years, a minor offense of one or two points will not count if you are able to avoid further violations in the following three months.

This table shows some of the more common offenses and their respective penalties.

POINTS	OFFENSE	PENALTY
15	drunken driving	fine and disqualification
15	driving under the influence of drugs	fine and disqualification
6	driving under the influence of alcohol	fine and suspension
12	speeding: more than 50 kph over the limit	fine and suspension
6	speeding: 30–50 kph over the limit	fine and suspension
3	speeding: 25–30 kph over the limit	¥18,000 fine
2	speeding: 20–25 kph over the limit	¥15,000 fine
1	speeding: 15–20 kph over the limit	¥12,000 fine
1	speeding: less than 15 kph over the limit	¥9,000 fine
2	going through a red light	¥9,000 fine
2	illegal passing	¥9,000 fine
2	not stopping at a railroad crossing	¥9,000 fine
2	stopping in a no-waiting area	¥12,000 fine
1	stopping in a no-parking area	¥10,000 fine
0	not carrying a driver's license	¥3,000 fine

(*Kōtsū Anzen Kyōkai,* as of October 1990)

Useful Words and Expressions

CITY AND WARD OFFICES

yakusho	government office
ku-yakusho	ward office
shi-yakusho	city office
Hōmu-shō	Ministry of Justice
kōmu-in	government worker
jichi-tai	local government
koseki	family register
tōroku-zumi shōmei-sho /jūmin-hyō	certificate of residence
han/inkan	name seal
inkan tōroku shōmei-sho	registration certificate for name seal
gaikoku-jin tōroku shōmei-sho	alien registration card
shimon	fingerprinting

IMMIGRATION

Nyūkoku Kanri Jimusho	Immigration Office
pasupōto/ryoken	passport
biza (zairyū-kikan) no kōshin	visa renewal
zairyū shikaku	residential status
hoshō-nin	sponsor
gensen chōshū shōmei-sho	certificate from employer showing amount of tax deducted
sai-nyūkoku	re-entry
sūji sai-nyūkoku kyoka	multiple re-entry permit

POLICE AND DRIVING

keisatsu	police
keisatsu-sho	police station
keikan	policeman
shiro-bai	police motorcycle
patokā	patrol car
unten menkyo-shō	driver's license
unten menkyo o kōshin suru	to renew a driver's license
chūsha ihan	parking offense

supiido ihan	speeding offense
inshu unten	drunken driving
ketsueki kensa	blood test
menkyo teishi	suspension of license
menkyo tori-keshi	disqualification from driving
ōtobai	motorcycle
gentsuki	motorcycle under 50cc, moped
nezumi-tori	radar trap
anzen unten	safe driving
kōtsū anzen	traffic safety

11   Gifts

The Japanese love to give things. Post offices give away tissues, pharmacies and photography shops ply customers with free samples and sundries, and most banks and department stores manage to produce balloons, toy banks, and other trinkets to pacify energetic children. At weddings, guests give donations inserted in beautiful envelopes when they arrive at the reception, and receive a present when they leave. When the Japanese travel, they often spend almost as much time shopping for gifts as they do on sightseeing. Travelers return from weekend trips with boxes of locally made cakes for their friends, relatives, and fellow office workers; at Narita Airport, they return fully weighted down with bags of presents. To take advantage of the Japanese predilection for buying gifts, some overseas souvenir shops sell handy ten-box packs of nuts and chocolates for tourists to distribute back home.

In Japan, a distinction is made between giving because you want to give and giving out of obligation. The difference is aptly illustrated on Valentine's Day, an occasion when women give chocolates to the men in their lives. If the chocolate is meant to be a sign of real affection, it is *hon-choko* (real chocolate); however, if it is given out of obligation, it is *giri-choko* (duty chocolate). Thus, teachers receive *giri-choko* from students, company employees from women in the office, and fathers from their daughters. The lucky men are those who receive *hon-choko* from lovers and secret admirers.

As a side note, the Japanese do not feel that they have to give Christmas gifts out of obligation, something that contrasts with what often happens in the West. In Japan, Christmas gifts are associated with romance and true affection, and, as of yet, there still do not exist any social rules dictating to whom they have to be given.

The two main gift-giving seasons are *o-chūgen* in July and *o-seibo* in December. During these two periods, the greatest volume of gift-giving occurs in the business world, where companies send gifts to clients to show that they are valued customers. In the private sector, a typical household's gift list includes a special teacher or tutor, the go-between at a wedding, and a family friend who used his or her influence to help find employment. Some people are given gifts because they have recently done or will do something for the family, and others are permanently on the gift list because the family values the long-term relationships.

The *o-chūgen* and *o-seibo* seasons, coinciding with the twice-yearly bonuses, are a bonanza for the department stores. Gifts for these two occasions usually range in price from two thousand yen to over twenty thousand yen, with the average price being about five thousand yen. Practical items like ham, soap, salad oil, and canned goods are the usual gifts, although more fancy products like imported wine and potted plants are gaining popularity.

You may want to keep in mind that in Japan, prestige is attached to where the gift is bought; that is why the same gift is better if it is wrapped in the paper of one department store rather than another. Another interesting point is that imported goods are often more highly valued than domestic goods.

While most people are undoubtedly pleased to receive their gifts, influential persons have tents pitched in their gardens to accommodate the deluge of gifts. These gifts are later sold off cheaply to bargain hunters.

Aside from the *o-chūgen* and *o-seibo* seasons, the milestones of life are also times when people give gifts. Birth, starting primary school, graduating from high school and university, building a house, and the sixtieth birthday are all occasions that are celebrated with gifts. In most instances, gifts are wrapped with special paper that specifies in beautiful calligraphy the occasion and the donor's name.

Money is often given on occasions like passing school entrance examinations, graduation, marriage, and sickness. The money is always cash, preferably new bills, and is put in special envelopes. These envelopes are available in stationery stores, supermarkets, and convenience stores; if you need help, the sales clerk will advise you which envelope is appropriate for which occasion.

Because giving gifts is only half the story, a word should be said about receiving gifts. According to Japanese etiquette, the recipient should give a return gift, *o-kaeshi,* which is equivalent to a third or a half of the value of the original gift. Thus, the new mother sends *o-kaeshi,* traditionally made of sugar, to all those who gave presents for her baby. People who have been ill send *o-kaeshi* for all the people who visited and brought gifts while they were sick. Likewise, the bride and groom arrange for their guests to be given gifts at the end of the wedding reception; these gifts are in fact *o-kaeshi* to the money that the guests presented when they arrived.

As stated before, the Japanese genuinely enjoy giving things. When you visit someone's home, you might be pressed with fruit, cakes, and even some of the dinner leftovers. The foreign visitor in particular may be given extravagant and very beautiful gifts. You do not need to reciprocate right away nor on the same scale, but you might want to take the time later to choose something special from your own country. Wine, china, ornaments, leather goods, a favorite brandy or whiskey—these all make gifts that please.

Having Something Gift-wrapped

Gifts for formal occasions are usually wrapped with a heavy white paper called *noshi-gami,* tied with stiff strings called *mizuhiki,* and decorated with a folded paper called *noshi.* Often the *noshi* and the *mizuhiki* are printed on the wrapping paper.

Clerks will neatly pack and wrap purchases using the store's paper. If you want your purchase specially gift-wrapped, make sure you tell the clerk that it is a present.

CUSTOMER:

Sumimasen. Kono urushi no o-bon, kudasai.

Excuse me. I'd like this lacquer tray, please.

CLERK:

Hai. O-tsukaimono desu ka?

Thank you. Is it a gift?

CUSTOMER:

Hai. Kekkon-iwai desukara, tsutsunde kudasai.

Yes. It's a wedding present so please wrap it appropriately.

CLERK:

Noshi o tsukemasu ka?

Shall I put the decorative folded paper on it?

CUSTOMER:

Iie. Kekkō desu. Kawari ni ribon o tsukete kudasai.

No, thank you. Please put a ribbon on it instead.

CLERK:

Hai, kashikomarimashita.

Certainly.

Offering a Gift

In formal situations, gifts are given usually after everyone has been seated, although sometimes in business, gifts are handed over just before leaving. When offering a gift wrapped in formal paper, make sure that the writing on the paper is right side up as it faces the recipient. Japanese always belittle the gifts they offer with phrases like:

• *Tsumaranai mono desu ga.*

This is a trifling thing.

• *Honno wazuka desu ga.*

It is only a small amount.

• *Honno kokoro-bakari no mono desu ga.*

It's only a small token.

In less formal situations, you might prefer to use one of the following examples:

• *Sukoshi desu ga, dōzo.*

This is just a very small token, but please (go ahead and take it).

• *Amerika no o-kashi desu. Dōzo, meshi-agatte mite kudasai.*

This is some candy from the United States. I hope you like it. (*lit.,* Please try it.)

• *Kanada no shashin-shū desu. Dōzo, goran kudasai.*

This is a book of photographs of Canada. I hope you enjoy looking at it. (*lit.,* Please look at it.)

• *Tezukuri no kukkii desu ga, dōzo tabete mite kudasai.*

169

I made these cookies myself. I hope you like them. (*lit.*, Please try them.)

· *Nani ga ii ka to mayoimashita ga, yōshu ga o-suki da to kikimashita node, kore o motte mairimashita. Kitto ki ni itte itadakeru to omoimasu.*

I didn't know what to give you but then I heard that you like Western liquors. So, this is what I brought. I'm sure you'll like it.

Opening a Gift

The following two examples will help you get around the Japanese custom of not opening a gift in the donor's presence:

· *Akete mite kudasai. Ki ni itte itadakeru to iin' desu ga.*

Please open it. I do hope you like it.

· *Akete mo ii desu ka?*

May I open it?

Expressing Thanks for a Gift

These expressions will convey your appreciation when you open a gift:

· *Subarashii!*

Wonderful!

- *Kirei desu ne!*
  It's really pretty!
- *Oishisō!*
  It looks delicious!
- *Wā, ureshii!*
  Ah, great! (used mostly by women)
- *Dōmo arigatō. Dai-kōbutsu desu.*
  Thank you. I'm very fond of this. (usually refering to food)
- *Ii kinen ni narimasu.*
  It will be a good souvenir.
- *Kanai mo yorokobimasu.*
  My wife will love it too.
- *Kyōshuku desu.*
  I am truly grateful.

In formal situations you may want to use the traditional phrase for receiving gifts:
- *Kore wa go-teinei ni arigatō gozaimashita.*
  How very nice of you. Thank you very much.

The next time you happen to talk to the person who gave you a gift, you can express your thanks once more with one of these phrases:
- *Senjitsu wa dōmo arigatō gozaimashita.*
  Thank you for (your gift) the other day.
- *Konaida wa dōmo gochisō-sama deshita. Taihen oishikatta desu.*
  Thank you for (your delicious gift) the other day. It was very good.

Gift Suggestions

This list will give you ideas as to what types of gifts are appropriate for different occasions.

VISITING PEOPLE FOR DINNER:
  Flowers, fruit, wine.

VISITING SOMEONE TO MAKE A REQUEST:
  Small box of cakes or candies.

VISITING AN IMPORTANT CLIENT:
Book, ornament, china, wine, or some practical item of high quality and good design. Giving something from your home country is a good idea.

VISITING FRIENDS:
Something homemade will always be appreciated.

SUMMER GIFTS:
Towel, soap, tea, iced tea or coffee set, fruit juice, beer, dried noodles like *sōmen* or *soba*, fruit, potted plant. These are gifts associated with coolness.

YEAR-END GIFTS:
Wine, whiskey, ham, sausage, butter, cheese, cyclamen plant. These are gifts that can be used over the Christmas and New Year holidays.

VISITING THE SICK:
Flowers, fruit, money.

AN EXHIBITION OR CONCERT:
Money, flowers, or box of cakes or candies.

Refusing a Gift

You do not have to accept unsolicited gifts. One tactful reason to give is that of working for the government.

DELIVERY MAN:
Takkyū-bin desu.
Delivery service.

RESIDENT: (after checking who the sender is)
Sumimasen ga, kōshoku ni tsuite imasu node, kore o uketoru wake ni wa ikanain' desu ga.
I'm sorry, but I can't accept this because I work for the government.

Telephoning to Say Thank You

Gifts should be acknowledged right away. A letter or postcard (*see* page 218) is the proper way to express thanks but a brief phone call will often suffice.

WOMAN:

Mitcheru desu ga, kyō wa o-todokemono o itadakimashite, arigatō gozaimashita.

This is Mrs. Mitchell. Your gift arrived today. Thank you very much.

FRIEND:

Iie, honno kokoro-bakari no mono desu.

It's only a small token.

WOMAN:

Chōdo hoshikatta mono desu. Arigatō gozaimashita. Mina-sama o-genki desu ka?

It was just what I wanted. Thank you very much. Is everyone fine?

FRIEND:

Hai. Okage-sama de.

Yes, thank you.

WOMAN:

Dewa, chikai uchi ni mata o-ai shimashō.

Well, let's get together soon.

FRIEND:

Sō shimashō. Waza-waza o-denwa arigatō gozaimashita.

Yes, let's do. Thank you for calling.

WOMAN:

Iie. Soredewa, gomen kudasai.

Not at all. Goodbye.

Expressions on Gift Papers

The following expressions, printed or written on gift papers and envelopes, cover the most common types of gifts.

御礼　　*o-rei* gift or fee for a service

御車代　*o-kurumadai* travel expense for a speaker, teacher, etc. Sometimes a euphemism for the fee itself.

寸志　　*sunshi* gift not connected with any particular occasion.

粗品　　*soshina* free gift from shops

寿	*kotobuki* gift for a wedding or other felicitous occasion
御祝	*o-iwai* gift for a wedding or other felicitous occasion
内祝	*uchi-iwai* gift to someone who gave you a gift for a wedding or other felicitous occasion
御餞別	*o-senbetsu* gift for someone who is going away
記念品	*kinen-hin* gift given to mark an occasion or achievement
御見舞	*o-mimai* gift or money given when visiting the sick
快気祝	*kaiki-iwai* gift to someone who visited you at the hospital
御年玉	*o-toshidama* money given at New Year to children
御年賀	*o-nenga* small gift given at New Year
御中元	*o-chūgen* summer gift given before mid-July
暑中見舞	*shochū-mimai* summer card, as well as gift, sent or given after mid-July
御誕生祝	*o-tanjō iwai* gift given to a new-born baby; also gift for an ordinary birthday
御入学祝	*go-nyūgaku iwai* gift or money for entering elementary school, junior high, high school, or college
御卒業祝	*go-sotsugyō iwai* gift or money for graduating
御霊前	*go-reizen* money given at funerals
御仏前	*go-butsuzen* money given at a Buddhist funeral service held forty-nine days after a death
御香典	*o-kōden* money given at a funeral
御供え	*o-sonae* offering to a home altar
志	*kokorozashi* return gift for a funeral offering

Useful Words and Expressions

okuri-mono	gift, often a small present such as a birthday gift
shinmotsu	gift, a word used mainly in advertisements and brochures
o-tsukaimono	gift to be delivered, a word used only by store clerks
o-chūgen	summer gift
o-seibo	year-end gift

gifuto	gift, usually either an *o-chūgen* or *o-seibo* gift
purezento	free gift
miyage	gift brought back from a trip, souvenir
o-kaeshi	return gift
noshi(-gami)	formal gift paper
kane o tsutsumu	wrapping money or inserting it in an envelope and then giving it as a gift

12 Weddings

PEOPLE STILL reminisce about old-fashioned weddings. In earlier times, the two families gathered at the bridegroom's home to wait for the bride, who usually arrived several hours behind schedule. The lively celebrations that followed the simple, private wedding ceremony went on late into the night, giving people a chance to drink away the hardships that marked their daily lives. After the initial celebrations, the festivities continued for a few days, during which several receptions were held to introduce the new couple to the various groups in the community.

Nowadays, both the ceremony and the reception are more likely to be held in a hotel or in a special wedding hall. At the reception, the bride and groom make their appearance illuminated by a spotlight, cut a huge cake in a swirl of dry ice, and change costumes two or even three times within the span of a few hours. The whole proceeding, which has become very commercialized, is available in a package plan that can cost millions of yen.

The marriage ceremony, still a private affair involving only the two families, usually takes place an hour or so before the reception in a small Shinto shrine within the hotel or wedding hall. The religious aspect of the ceremony is a recent phenomenon; in fact, the first recorded Shinto wedding ceremony occurred in 1873. In a Shinto wedding, the ceremony begins with a priest waving his staff of white paper strands over the assembly as he invokes the gods with prayers. After the couple exchange wedding rings, the groom reads a pledge that is similar to the vows of a Christian marriage. To solemnize the marriage, the couple sip saké from a set of three flat cups.

Christian weddings, performed with the traditional vows and hymns, are currently in vogue. In most cases, the bride and groom have no connection with any particular church.

If you are invited to a Shinto wedding, the invitation most likely will be only for the reception. The reception, which is called the *hirō-en* and means "announcement," is supposed to formally announce to society that the couple have been united. Even today if the two families live far apart, receptions usually are held in both communities.

Giving money at weddings is a custom that started in poorer

days when friends and relatives of the two families contributed to lighten the financial burden of the wedding. The money that guests take to weddings nowadays is meant to cover the cost of the meal and the gift they will receive, and hopefully to leave some left over. The going rate is twenty thousand yen per guest but if you are invited to a wedding, it is best to talk with Japanese friends who are going. Some weddings, especially those financed by the young couple themselves, are on a shared-cost basis, or *kaihi-sei*, and everyone is asked to bring a certain amount. The beautiful envelopes that are used for wedding contributions are sold at stationery stores and supermarkets everywhere.

People do give wedding presents either instead of or as well as money. If you decide to give a present, it should be delivered to the bride or the groom before the wedding. One good idea is to give a small, personal gift beforehand, and after consultation with others attending the wedding, to take a modest sum of money to hand over at the reception.

The wedding reception is a ceremony in itself. The bride and groom sit in front of a gold screen and on a dais facing the guests. The couple are flanked by the go-between couple, who in olden times would have made the match but who now are more likely the bridegroom's mentor at work and his or her spouse. After announcing that the marriage ceremony has been solemnized, the go-between gives the personal histories of both partners. Then there are speeches, often by the bosses of the bride and the groom, stressing the reliability of the two partners and expressing hopes that the marriage will last. These speeches tend to be stiff and formal, and not until the toast, which precedes the feast, does the party begin.

Replying to an Invitation

A reply card is usually sent with the invitation. Fill in your name, address, and whether you will attend or not. When you mail the card back, you should cross out the respectful prefix *go*, which precedes your name. You can also add a few words of congratulation, or in the case of a refusal, a short explanation and apology.

- *Shusseki: Yorokonde shusseki sasete itadakımasu.*
  Will attend: I look forward to attending.
- *Kesseki: Tōjitsu wa Amerika ni kaette orimasu node shitsurei sasete itadakimasu. Omedetō gozaimasu. O-shiawase ni.*
  Will not attend: I will be back in the United States that day and regret that I will not be able to attend. Congratulations. I wish you much happiness.

Arriving at the Reception

On the day of the reception, dress in your finery; *heifuku*, which means "everyday clothes," on an invitation should not be taken literally. Because there are preliminaries to be completed, you should arrive at the venue about fifteen minutes before the announced time. At the reception desk, present your money, which should be enclosed in the special envelope used for weddings, and sign the guest book. If you have sent a gift instead of giving money, explain the situation to the receptionist:

- *O-iwai wa okurimashita node.*
  I have already sent a gift.

As you enter the banquet room, greet the bride and groom, the go-betweens, and both sets of parents, who will all be waiting at the entrance. Bow or shake hands and offer your congratulations to all concerned:

- *Omedetō gozaimasu.*
  Congratulations.

You can also compliment the bride:

- *O-kirei desu ne.*
  You look lovely.

Leaving the Reception

The same group who welcomed you to the reception room will see you out as you leave. It is then appropriate to wish the bride and groom every happiness:

• *O-shiawase ni.*
I wish you all the happiness.

Then you should thank and/or compliment the parents:
• *Subarashii hirō-en deshita.*
It was a wonderful reception.

Wedding Speeches

The formal atmosphere at the beginning of a Japanese wedding reception can be unnerving to anyone who has to make a speech. Just remember that the first few speeches, the introduction by the go-between, and the speeches of the main guests are ceremonial. If you are the boss of the bride or the groom, you may well be one of the first to speak. If so, your speech must be well prepared.

Comments alluding to marriage as being one foot in the grave and jokes of that ilk are out of place at this stage of a Japanese wedding. The whole tone must be felicitous. It is customary to eulogize the bride and groom as paragons of beauty, talent, and intelligence. Check your speech too for taboo words (p. 187).

A toast comes after the last main speech, and this is followed by more frank and amusing speeches given by friends of the bride and groom. Some incident that throws light on the bride or groom's personality, or some explanation of how they met provides a welcome contrast to the polite clichés that characterize the formal speeches before the toast.

Foreigners are frequently invited to Japanese weddings and asked to give speeches even though they may have only a casual acquaintance with the bride or the groom; the intention is often to give the wedding an "international" flavor. If you are giving a speech, start with some conventional words of congratulation and speak slower than usual so the audience can adjust to the fact that you are speaking Japanese. Although jokes should be used with discretion, a few phrases or epigrams in English often prove popular. You can even opt out of speaking Japanese altogether and sing a song instead. Do not dismiss this as out of hand because the audience certainly will enjoy it.

181

Giving a Formal Speech

This formal speech, suitable if you are a main guest, shows the kind of sentiments one is expected to express. After a few words of congratulation, the speaker, who is the bride's boss, introduces himself and compliments the couple. The speaker continues by praising the bride's personality and accomplishments. Although he finishes with a play on words, he is careful to maintain a formal tone throughout his speech.

Yūji-san, Yumi-san, soshite go-ryōke no minasama-gata, omedetō gozaimasu. Kokoro kara o-yorokobi o mōshi-agemasu.

Watakushi wa shinpu no tsutomete oraremasu ABC Ginkō no Nihon manējā no Mitcheru de gozaimasu. Honjitsu wa o-maneki itadakimashite kōei ni zonjimasu.

Honjitsu wa Yumi-san no utsukushii hana-yome sugata o haiken itashimashite, hontō ni kangeki shite imasu.

Yumi-san wa watakushi-domo no kaisha ni haitte sannen ni narimasu ga, shigoto o sukkari masutā shi, donna koto ga atte mo shikkari yatte kudasaru kata desu. Soshite itsumo akaruku tanoshisō ni shigoto o konashi, sono utsukushii hoho-emi to te-bayai shigoto-buri ga waga gyōmu-bu no sasae ni mo natte imasu. Kongo-tomo wagasha ni chikara o kashite kudasaru koto o kitai shite orimasu.

Shikashi sore dake dewa naku, kaisha igai demo hijō ni katsuyaku sare, tasai na ojōsan de aru to iu koto wa minasama no go-shōchi no tōri desu. O-cha, tenisu nado, wayō dochira mo konasu, masa ni ima no kokusai shakai ni fusawashii sainō no mochi-nushi de arimasu.

Yūji-san ni wa, Yumi-san no go-ryōshin ga ika ni taisetsu ni sodaterareta ka o-wakari no koto to omoimasu. Itsumade-mo kanojo o aishi, daiji ni shite kudasaru koto o kokoro kara o-negai itashimasu.

Enman na katei o kizuku tame no seiyō no otoko no chie o oshiemashō. Kantan na koto desu. Sore wa okusan o tatete, daiji ni suru koto desu. Aruiwa, waga ginkō gyōkai no hyōgen o karimasu to, kekkon wa hitotsu no chōki tōshi de ari, aijō o kotsu-kotsu tsumi-tatenai to manki niwa narimasen.

Dōka, o-futaritomo "tanki" o okosanaide, shōrai no ōki na minori o uke-totte kudasai.

Kyō wa hontō ni omedetō gozaimasu.

Yuji, Yumi, and the Sato and Ito families, please accept my sincere congratulations. My name is Mitchell and I am the manager of the Japan office of the ABC Bank, where the bride is employed. It is a great honor to be here today. I am very moved to see Yumi on her wedding day looking so lovely.

Since joining our company three years ago, Yumi has mastered her work so well that we can rely on her whatever the circumstances. Moreover, she always manages to work happily and with a cheerful expression. Her beautiful smile and her efficiency help support our office. I hope she will continue with our company in the future.

Yumi is also extremely active outside the company; I am sure you are all aware that she is a very talented young lady. She enjoys both Japanese and Western things like the tea ceremony and tennis, and she possesses talents eminently suited to today's international society.

I am certain that Yuji knows what a precious daughter Yumi is to her parents. I sincerely hope he will love her and care for her always.

Let me tell you how men in the West attain marital bliss. It's simple. Defer to your wife and care for her. Or, to borrow a saying from our banking business, marriage is a long-term investment that doesn't reach maturity unless there are regular additional installments of affection.

May you both temper your impatience,* and enjoy the fruits of your investment for many years to come.

As for today, my sincerest congratulations!

* This is a pun on the word *tanki*, which means both "impatient" and "short-term."

Giving an Informal Speech (1)

This lively, cheerful speech is given by a female friend of the bride.

Yumi-san, Itō-san, omedetō gozaimasu. Kyō wa o-maneki itadaki, arigatō gozaimashita. Watakushi wa, Yumi-san to onaji kaisha de hataraite orimasu Janetto Chen de gozaimasu. Hon Kon shusshin desu.

Kyō wa, kono ichi-nenkan no Yumi-san no henshin ni tsuite o-hanashi shitai to omoimasu. Yumi-san wa shokuji ni amari kyōmi o shimesu hito dewa arimasen deshita. O-hiru yasumi ni wa fāsuto fūdo o satto tabete kaimono ni iku ka, aruiwa kissaten de yukkuri to o-shaberi o shite imashita.

Shikashi, rokkagetsu mae ni, Yumi-san wa kawarimashita. Shokuji to o-ryōri ni taihen kyōmi o motsu yō ni natta no desu. Ii resutoran o sagashi-dashite, o-hiru yasumi ni wa iroiro na tokoro o annai shite kuremashita. Mata Chūgoku ryōri ni tsuite iroiro watashi ni kiku yō ni narimashita. Aru hi itame-mono o kaisha made motte kite, watashi ni aji-mi o sasemashita.

Saisho wa kono henka o rikai dekimasen deshita ga, sūkagetsu mae ni subete ga akiraka ni narimashita. Itō-san to no majika ni sematta kekkon ga sono haikei ni arimashita.

Eigo dewa "Otoko no kokoro ni tsūjiru no wa ibukuro de aru" to iu koto-waza ga arimasu. Chūgoku-jin mo otoko no kokoro o tsunagi-tomeru no wa ibukuro de aru to shinjite imasu. Dōka, futari de itsumade-mo oishii o-ryōri o tanoshinde kudasai.

*Yumi-san wa kappatsu na, akarui josei desu. Soshite, kyō goran
no yō ni utsukushii josei demo arimasu. Itō-san, Yumi-san, hontō ni
kyō wa omedetō gozaimasu. Itsumade-mo o-shiawase ni.*

Congratulations, Yumi and Yuji. I'm very glad to be here
today. My name is Janet Chen, I'm from Hong Kong, and
I work with Yumi at the same company.

I want to tell you today about the change I have witnessed
in Yumi over the last year. Yumi was never one who was
very interested in food. Lunch break would be a quick bite
at a fast-food restaurant before going shopping or having a
leisurely chat in a coffee shop.

Then, about six months ago something strange happened
to Yumi. She became inordinately fond of food and cooking.
She would search out good restaurants for us to go to for lunch.
And she would quiz me about Chinese cooking. Once she even
made some stir-fry and brought it to work for me to taste!
At first I couldn't understand this change, but then a few
months ago all was revealed. Her impending marriage to Yuji
was the reason.

In English there is a saying: The way to a man's heart
is through his stomach. May I add that we Chinese also
believe that the way to keep a man is through his stomach!
May you both enjoy good food for many years to come.

Yumi is a lively and cheerful person, and as we can all
see today, also very beautiful. Congratulations to you both.
I wish you all the happiness.

Giving an Informal Speech (2)

This speech is given by a male English teacher who was invited
by the bridegroom.

*Yūji-san, Yumi-san, go-kekkon omedetō. Watakushi wa shinro
Itō-kun no Ei-kaiwa kyōshi no Jakku Kūpā desu. Kyō wa o-maneki
itadaki, arigatō gozaimasu. Hajimete Nihon no kekkon-shiki ni
shusseki shimasu node, kore wa subarashii keiken desu.*

185

Sate, toki wa sakunen no Shichigatsu yokka, Amerika Dokuritsu Kinen-bi. ABC Ei-kaiwa Gakkō de wa "Ingurisshu onrii" no jikan desu. Aru wakai Nihon-jin no otoko ga yūki o motte Nihon no kawaii musume-san ni Eigo de iroiro shitsumon shite imasu. Kaiwa wa migoto ni hazumimasu. Nan-to subarashii Eigo no jōtatsu darō to watashi wa kangeki shimashita. Kono toki no futari ga hoka demo arimasen. Genzai watashi-tachi no mae de sakan ni terete iru shinrō-shinpu na no desu. Sono ato watashi wa Amerika e ikimashita kara, dō natta no ka yoku shirimasen ga, kare to kanojo wa sono natsu no aida ni o-atsuku natta yō desu.

Amerika-jin no tomodachi ni yoreba, kekkon wa atsui o-furo no yō na mono da sō desu. Haitte shimau to, sore-hodo atsui mono dewa arimasen! Shikashi karera wa Nihon no oidaki-buro no koto wa shiranai no desu! Dōka, Yūji, Yumi. Nihon-jin no ai no bānā o tsukatte, o-futari no kekkon o itsumade-mo atsui mono ni shite kudasai. Dōzo, o-shiawase ni.

Yuji, Yumi, congratulations on your wedding day! I am Yuji's English teacher, and my name is Jack Cooper. Thank you very much for inviting me today. This is the first Japanese wedding I have ever attended and it is a wonderful experience.

Let me take you back to last year's Fourth of July, America's Independence Day. It's "English only" time at the ABC School of English Conversation. A young Japanese man bravely asks a sweet Japanese woman questions in English. The conversation is animated. I marvel at their progress in English. Lo and behold, these two were none other than the bride and groom, the two who are looking extremely embarrassed right now! Soon after that I went to the States and don't really know what happened, but it seems that things really heated up between them during that summer.

My American friends tell me that marriage is like a hot bath; it's not so hot once you're in it! But they don't know about the Japanese bath, which can be heated up whenever it cools. Yuji, Yumi, may you use the Japanese burner of love to heat your marriage forever. I wish you all the happiness.

Making a Toast

The toast marks the end of the ceremonial speeches and the start of the wedding feast. If you wish, add a few words of introduction to the following toast.

Dewa kanpai no ondo o torasete itadakimasu. Yūji-san, Yumi-san, hontō ni kyō wa omedetō gozaimasu. Sara ni, Itō-ke, Satō-ke no masu-masu no go-han'ei, awasete go-rinseki no minasama no go-kenshō o kinen itashimashite, kanpai o itashimasu! Kanpai!

I would like to propose a toast:
To Yuji and Yumi on this happy day. To the prosperity of the Ito and Sato families, and to the good health of us all. Congratulations!

Taboo Words

The use of certain words, *imi kotoba,* during weddings is believed to be unlucky. This superstition dates from the Heian period, became widespread in the fifteenth century, and survives even today. These words are shunned because of their associations with an unsuccessful marriage. For example, *kiru* (to cut) is not used because of its connotations with *en o kiru* (to break off a relationship); *kyonen* (last year) because it is written with the character meaning to leave; and *kuri-kaesu* (to repeat) because it hints at divorce and remarriage.

Following is a list of common taboo words, and for some of them, appropriate substitutions.

TABOO WORD	MEANING	SUBSTITUTE WITH
kyonen	last year	*sakunen*
kaeru	to leave	*chūza suru* or *shitsurei suru*
kiru	to cut	*naifu o ireru*
owari	end, close	*o-hiraki*
saru	to leave	avoid
wakareru	to part	avoid
modoru	to return	avoid
yaburu	to break	avoid
kuri-kaesu	to repeat	avoid

187

akiru	to become bored	avoid
tabi-tabi	again and again	avoid
mō ichido	once more	avoid

Sending a Telegram

If you cannot attend a wedding, you might consider sending a telegram. In Japan, dial 115, ask for telegrams by saying *Denpō o uchitain' desu ga,* and then give your name and number. The operator will call you back to ask you what you want to say in the telegram.

Here are some sample telegrams; you can find others in a Japanese telephone directory.

- *Go-kekkon omedetō gozaimasu.*
  Congratulations on your marriage.
- *Go-kekkon o shukushi, sue-nagaku sachi ōkare to inorimasu.*
  Congratulations on your marriage, and much happiness always.
- *Omedetō. Suteki na o-futari ni kanpai.*
  Congratulations. A toast to a wonderful couple!
- *Yorokobi ippai shiawase ippai no ima no kimochi itsumade-mo.*
  May the joy and happiness you feel today last forever.

Epigrams

An epigram may be appropriate to include in a card, telegram, or speech.

- Marriage has many pains, but celibacy has few pleasures. (Samuel Johnson)
  Kekkon seikatsu wa ōku no kutsū o motsu ga, dokushin seikatsu wa yorokobi o motanai.
- A good husband makes a good wife. (Robert Burton)
  Yoki otto wa yoki tsuma o tsukuru.
- Women are meant to be loved, not understood. (Oscar Wilde)
  Josei wa rikai subeki mono dewa naku, ai subeki mono de aru.
- Keep your eyes wide open before marriage and half-shut afterwards. (Anonymous)
  Kekkon-mae wa ryōme o ake, kekkon shitara katame o tsubure.

Useful Words and Expressions

kon-yaku	engagement
yuinō	betrothal present or ceremony
kekkon iwai	wedding present or money donation
hikide-mono	gift for a guest
kekkon-shiki	wedding
Shinzen kekkon-shiki	Shinto wedding
Butsuzen kekkon-shiki	Buddhist wedding
Kirisuto-kyō kekkon-shiki	Christian wedding
kekkon hirō-en	wedding reception
(kekkon) kinen shashin	wedding photograph
shinrō/hana-muko	bridegroom
shinpu/hana-yome	bride
o-nakōdo	go-between (conversational)
go-baishakunin	go-between (formal)
go-ryōke	the two families
shuhin	main guest
san-san-ku-do	part of the marriage rite in which the couple exchanges saké cups
o-ironaoshi	bride's change of costume
shukuji	wedding speech
shukuden	congratulatory telegram

13 Funerals

JAPANESE FUNERALS reflect a number of the positive aspects of Japan's traditional, group-oriented society. On hearing of a death, friends and acquaintances who live nearby rush to offer their condolences, often showing great emotion not normally associated with the reserved Japanese. Close relatives take several days off work to help with the funeral arrangements, and children are automatically excused from school for a prescribed number of days. The wives in the neighborhood may take over the kitchen and prepare mainly vegetarian food for the family in mourning and for the many visitors who come to pay their respects. During this period, the house can be a hive of activity. In fact, there is even a saying that a grandparent's funeral is a grandchild's festival, which in Japanese is *Jiji-baba no sōshiki wa mago no matsuri*.

Generally speaking, when a person dies in Japan, the body is brought as soon as possible to the house and is laid out with the head to the north, a direction usually avoided when sleeping. The body is dressed in a white kimono worn right over left instead of the usual left over right, and given a purse containing the fare for the ferry across the Buddhist River Styx, *Sanzu no Kawa*, and a walking stick and straw sandals for the arduous journey to paradise. The wake takes place the same day or the next day and is a religious service starting about six or seven in the evening.

The funeral, usually occurring the following day, is a brief, private service held in the home, at a temple, or at a funeral home. After the funeral, neighbors dressed in black clothes line the street outside to see the deceased off to the crematory. (In Japan, cremation is the norm.) The family returns home from the crematory with the urn of ashes and places it on a specially erected altar. A general memorial service is usually held three or four days later, although occasionally it is held weeks or even months later. According to Buddhist practices, mourning lasts for forty-nine days, and sometime during this period the ashes are interred in the family grave.

If the deceased was a close friend or a business acquaintance, you must decide whether to attend the wake, the memorial service, or both. For the memorial service, mourning clothes should be worn. This means black suit and tie for men, and black suit or dress with plain, black shoes and purse for women. Unless you have heard that offerings will not be accepted, *go-jitai mōshiagemasu,* you should prepare an offering in a special envelope used for funerals. These envelopes, which are either made out of a stiff white paper folded and tied elegantly with black and silver strings or, especially nowadays, just printed with this design, are sold at stationery stores and convenience stores. Those marked *go-reizen* 御霊前 (before the spirit of the departed) are for any funeral regardless of religion, and those marked *go-butsuzen* 御仏前 (before the Buddha) are for Buddhist memorial services after the forty-ninth day, when the spirit has attained enlightenment. The amount you give depends on your relationship to the deceased; most people enclose three, five, or ten thousand yen. You will probably receive a gift in return for your offering.

When you arrive at the memorial service, present your donation at the reception table and write your name and address in the guest book. Next, turn to the family of the deceased, who will be lined up to receive the mourners. You can either bow, shake hands, or express your regret in English or Japanese. Anything that comes naturally is acceptable.

The room where the service is held will have a photograph of the deceased and, under it, the box containing the urn of ashes.

[envelope for funerals]

御霊前

コナーズ

The whole display will be richly decorated with flowers. The service begins with a religious ceremony lasting for about thirty minutes and is followed by short eulogies addressed to the deceased. After speeches of thanks by the chairman of the funeral committee and by the chief mourner, the general mourners file up to offer either incense or flowers. At Shinto funerals, which are rare, branches of *sakaki* are offered.

The Japanese consider attending funerals more important than anything, even work. This attitude is reflected in the Labor Standards Act, which stipulates that absence for mourning be calculated separately from one's annual paid leave. Also, Japanese frequently attend services for a parent or even a grandparent of an acquaintance, even though they may never have met the deceased. If the deceased was your friend or was a business acquaintance with whom you had regular contact, you should at least make an effort to attend the memorial service.

Being Informed of a Death

A mutual acquaintance will probably inform you by telephone that someone has died. You might want to find out what that person intends to do and then ask if you may go along.

BUSINESSMAN:

Takahashi desu ga. Anō, Yamada-san no otōsan ga kyō nakunararetan' desu yo.

Hello. This is Takahashi. Did you hear that Yamada's father died today?

COLLEAGUE:

Sore-wa sore-wa.

I am sorry to hear that.

BUSINESSMAN:

Sore-de, o-tsuya wa kyō no roku-ji-han ni go-jitaku de okonawaremasu ga, kokubetsu-shiki wa jūyokka no gogo ni-ji ni Dai-ichi Kaikan de okonau yotei da sō desu.

The wake will be held today at 6:30 at the house and the memorial service at 2:00 on the fourteenth at the Daiichi Hall.

COLLEAGUE:

Sō desu ka. Arigatō gozaimasu. Takahashi-san wa dō shimasu ka?

Thank you for letting me know. What do you plan to do?

BUSINESSMAN:

Sō desu ne. Kokubetsu-shiki dake ni deyō to omotte imasu ga...

Well, I thought I'd just go to the memorial service.

COLLEAGUE:

Sō desu ka? Ja, sashi-tsukae ga nakereba, issho ni itte mo ii deshō ka?

I see. If it's not a problem, could I go with you?

BUSINESSMAN:

Sō desu ne. Jā, ichi-ji yonjuppun ni kaijō no robii de aimashō.

Not at all. Let's meet in the lobby of the Daiichi Hall at 1:40.

COLLEAGUE:

Arigatō gozaimasu. O-negai shimasu.

Thank you. I appreciate it. (*lit.,* I request.)

BUSINESSMAN:

Shitsurei shimasu.

Goodbye.

Visiting the Home

If a neighbor, a close friend, or a relative of a close friend dies, you can go at any time to the house to express your condolences. Take a gift of flowers or fruit; in return, you will probably receive a small gift. Tell the florist or fruit dealer for what purpose the flowers or fruit will be used:

• *Kore de chiisa na mori-bana o tsukutte kudasai. Butsudan ni agetain' desu ga.*

Please make a small arrangement out of these flowers. They're for a home altar.

• *Kudamono o mori-awasete kudasai. Butsudan ni agetain' desu ga.*

Please make up a basket of fruit. They're for a home altar.

When you reach the house, you will be ushered into a room that the undertakers have transformed with yards of white material. There will be an altar, a photograph of the deceased, candles, and offerings of fruit and cakes. You should bow to the bereaved, present your gift, and say the following:

- *Goshūshō-sama de gozaimasu. Go-reizen ni dōzo.*
  You have my deepest sympathy. This is for the spirit of the departed.

Then proceed to the altar. After bowing your head in prayer, look briefly at the photograph of the deceased. If you wish, you can offer incense. Bow once more, turn to the family, bow, and leave.

Offering Incense

At both a wake or a memorial service, people offer incense when paying respects to the deceased. If incense sticks are used, follow this procedure:
1. Bow. Take one or more sticks of incense and light them from the candle.
2. Fan sticks with the left hand to extinguish. Do not blow!
3. Stand the sticks separately in the incense burner.
4. Bow once more.

If powdered incense is used, bow, take a pinch of incense and sprinkle it over the incense burner, and bow once more.

Expressing Your Condolences

If you watch the ladies in their black kimono, you can see that
bows can be far more eloquent than words. Still, you may want to
express your grief in words.

• *Kono tabi wa goshūshō-sama de gozaimashita.*
  Please accept my deepest sympathy.
• *Kono tabi wa tonda koto de.*
  It was so unexpected.
• *Haya-sugite hontō ni zannen deshita.*
  It is most unfortunate. She was far too young.
• *Rippa na kata deshita.*
  He was a fine man.
• *Taihen goshūshō-sama de gozaimashita. Watakushi ni nani-ka dekiru
  koto ga arimashitara, go-enryo naku o-mōshitsuke kudasai.*
  Please accept my deepest sympathy. If there is anything I
  can do, please do not hesitate to ask.

Sending a Telegram

In the past, telegrams of condolence were sent by people who were
unable to hurry immediately to the house of the deceased. Sending
condolence telegrams has become even more widespread today. If
you can read Japanese, the procedure for sending them is very
easy. After you have looked over the samples at the back of a
Japanese telephone directory, dial 115 and quote the number of
the telegram you want to send. The text of the telegram will be
similiar to the following examples.

• *Tsutsushinde aitō no i o hyōshimasu.*
  Please accept my condolences. (*lit.,* I respectfully express my
  condolences.)
• *Go-seikyo o itami, tsutsushinde o-kuyami mōshi-agemasu.*
  I grieve over your loss and offer my respectful sympathy.
• *Go-seikyo o itami, go-meifuku o o-inori mōshi-agemasu.*
  I grieve over your loss and pray that he rests in peace.
• *Go-sonpusama (go-bodōsama) no go-seikyo o itami, tsutsushinde
  o-kuyami mōshi-agemasu.*

I grieve over the passing of your father (mother) and offer my respectful sympathy.

• *Arishi-hi no o-sugata o shinobi, kokoro kara go-meifuku o o-inori mōshi-agemasu.*

I cherish memories of the departed and sincerely pray that she rests in peace.

Offering Branches of Sakaki

In a Shinto memorial service, the priest hands each person a branch of the *sakaki* to place on the altar. The procedure for placing the branch on the altar is as follows:

1. Bow once.
2. Turn the branch around clockwise and place it with the stem toward the altar.
3. Bow twice and *silently* clap twice.
4. Bow once more.

Writing a Letter of Sympathy

Although sending a letter of sympathy is not a Japanese custom, a letter can often be a great consolation.

Go-shujin no totsuzen no go-seikyo o ukagai, taihen na odoroki to kanashimi o kanjimashita. Sengetsu o-hanashi shita bakari na noni, kono yo o satte shimawareta to wa totemo shinjiraremasen.

Go-shujin wa rippa na kata de, mata ii tomo deshita. Shigoto ni wa kibishii kata deshita ga, ningen-sei ga yutaka de, itsumo hito no tame ni isshō-kenmei tsukushite imashita. Nihon ni kite kara mada hi ga asai watashi wa go-shujin ni taihen o-sewa ni nari, sono koto wa itsumade-mo wasurenai deshō.

Go-seikyo o itami, tsutsushinde o-kuyami mōshi-agemasu.

I was most shocked and saddened to hear of the sudden death of your husband. It is very hard to believe that he is no longer with us; it was only one month ago that I had talked to him.

Your husband was a fine man and a good friend. Although he was strict at work, he always had time for people. I will forever be grateful for the unstinting help he gave me during my early days in Japan.

Please accept my most sincere condolences in your bereavement.

Useful Words and Expressions

tsuya	wake
sōgi/sōshiki	funeral
kokubetsu-shiki	funeral service for general mourners
sōgi ni sanretsu suru	to attend a funeral
Fukō ga atta.	Someone has died. (*lit.*, Something unfortunate has happened.)
hōyō/hōji	Buddhist memorial service
o-kuyami	condolence
chōden	condolence telegram
kōden	offering of money at a funeral
kōden dorobō	thief, posing as a mourner, who steals funeral offerings
gasshō	Buddhist prayer position for the hands
Go-kiritsu kudasai.	Please stand.
o-kyō	Buddhist sutra

senkō	incense stick
senkō o ageru	to offer an incense stick
shōkō suru	to offer powdered incense
butsudan	Buddhist home altar
izoku	the bereaved
ko-~	the late ~
o-bōsama/o-shōsan	Buddhist priest
moshu	chief mourner
sōgi iin-chō	chairman of the funeral committee
sōgi-ya	funeral director
hitsugi/o-kan	coffin
shukkan	carrying the coffin out of the house
reikyū-sha	hearse
kasō suru	to cremate
kasō-ba	crematory
o-kotsu	the ashes
kibiki kyūka	absence from work or school due to mourning
chōji	obituary
isshū-ki	service on the first anniversary of a death
sankai-ki	service on the second anniversary of a death
kaimyō	Buddhist name given to a person after death

Ihai-mochi

Ihai are the wooden memorial tablets kept in Buddhist home altars. Each *ihai* tablet bears the posthumous name of a deceased relative. *Ihai-mochi*, which means "keeper of the memorial tablets," is a term used to refer to the oldest son. People may call an oldest son *ihai-mochi* to remind him that one day he will inherit the family altar, the memorial tablets, and the responsibility of carrying on the family name. The oldest son may also use *ihai-mochi* to show that he is resigned to carrying out his family responsibilities.

14 Speeches

WITH THE EXCEPTION of lectures, *kōen*, speeches in Japan are seldom original. In most cases, everybody pretty much knows at the outset what to expect. This is especially true with the short introductory speech referred to as the *go-aisatsu*, which literally means "greeting." Regardless of whether the *go-aisatsu* is a congratulatory message at a reception or an animated pep talk in front of the whole company, people expect the speech to include certain set expressions and to have a certain style and form. If the speech departs from the norm, it might be judged odd and unsettling.

In any given ceremony, each of the many speeches has a specific function, e.g., introducing the speakers, stating goals and objectives, thanking people for coming, giving the toast, and closing the ceremony. Sometimes various guests, starting with the VIPs and moving downward, will be called upon to say a few words at large business receptions. In many cases, the less important speeches become the background music against which the guests help themselves to the food served at the elegantly prepared buffet tables.

Let us put serious speeches and lectures aside for a moment and first deal with speeches given at social functions. If you are asked to give a speech, think of it as one piece in the overall structure of the ceremony. Decide whether your speech is a keystone, a supporting block, or a decoration, and adapt the tone and length accordingly. Unless you are the main speaker, great thoughts or verbal pyrotechnics are not expected and probably are out of place.

The very fact that you are standing up and making a speech in Japanese is quite enough to impress people. In most instances, you do not have to strain yourself to make your presentation unique. Thus, you should try not to spoil your speech by making jokes about Japan, giving one personal opinion after another, or delivering a flood of witty comments or ironic barbs. Too many of these informal comments often will just make a Japanese audience feel uncomfortable.

This is not to say that your speech has to be without humor. Once you have established a properly serious tone and have said all the right things, a little levity can give spark to your speech, so long as it is not at the expense of anyone present. In fact, if you can manage it, a few verbal jokes and puns in Japanese can be very effective. A word of caution though: regardless of whether said in English or in Japanese, Western jokes seldom go over well with the Japanese.

A good speaker in Japan always has lots of thanks to give. Even if he really is the person with all the power, he will say that everyone has been learning and growing together, stress that he has constantly borrowed other people's strengths and wisdom, and protest that he could not do anything without the audience's help and cooperation. Whatever the activity, whether it is managing a neighborhood baseball team or taking over an American bank, a good speaker will insist that it is an effort, *doryoku*, to which everyone can contribute with his or her determination, *ketsui*, devotion, *kenshin*, and tenacity, *shūnen*. Above all, he will stress that the whole activity will be done wholeheartedly, *isshō-kenmei*, with each person giving all that he or she can give, *ganbaru* (or, in more formal settings, *zenshin o agete* or *doryoku shite mairu*).

Furthermore, while the audience may not particularly want to know what you think of your own home country, they will surely be interested to hear what you have noticed about them. Talking of things that are familiar to your audience is the surest way of paying them a compliment. Flattering the person in whose honor you are speaking is, of course, a very good idea. Perhaps you could also think of some local custom, event, or cuisine, and somehow work it in your speech. Sharing your views about a local topic will show your audience that you have taken the time to learn something about them.

Now let us look at serious speeches and lectures. Since people are probably spending time and/or money to hear your opinions, you should not disappoint them by delivering a speech with no substance. The biggest danger is making your speech too complicated. Whether you are speaking in Japanese or through an interpreter, you should expect that twenty percent of what you say will not get through. For one thing, a speech is not an essay and unless you have an uncommon mastery of Japanese, subtle meanings and nuances will neither be understood nor appreciated by the audience. Therefore, keep your sentences short and punchy and organize your speech so that it concentrates on just a few main points. Your main ideas are often best listed as "Five Points" or "Four Principles," and you should enumerate them, elaborate on them, and then recapitulate them.

One final word of advice: do not be discouraged if your audience adopts a somnolent posture within seconds after you begin your speech. It can happen to any speaker. Sympathize with them, since they may be a drafted audience, and remember that they may not be used to hearing original, thought-provoking speeches. If what you have to say is really important, try to make sure in advance that the speech is available to the audience in written form, or that the press is there and primed with a printed synopsis of the major points. In the majority of cases, however, the fact that you are contributing to the ceremonial procedures of the occasion is the most important thing.

Introducing Yourself

A typical gathering begins with individual introductions, *jiko shōkai*. The basic introduction consists of your name and, most important, your affiliation. You can also explain where you come from, how long you have been in Japan, your impressions of the country, your interests, and so on. At informal company parties, you can gain instant popularity by showing off your singing ability.

- *Monbu-shō ryūgaku-sei no Janetto Furai desu. Dōzo yoroshiku.*
  I'm Janet Fry and I'm a Ministry of Education scholarship student. I'm pleased to be here.

- *ABC Ginkō no Jon Sumisu desu. Umare wa Amerika no Tekisasu-shū de, rokkagetsu mae ni Nihon ni kimashita. Rāmen bakkari tabete, jūdō o yatte, san-kiro yasemashita!*
  I'm John Smith of the ABC Bank. I'm from Texas and I came to Japan six months ago. I've taken up judo, lived on ramen, and lost three kilos!

- *Eigyō no Kāson desu. Kuni no uta o utaimasu. "Teneshii Warutsu" desu.*

I'm Carson from sales. I'd like to sing you a song from my home state. It's called "The Tennessee Waltz."

Beginning a Speech

Although the body of a speech is fine in a normal, conversational style using the -*masu* endings of verbs, there are conventional, formal phrases which should be used at the beginning and end. The following two examples will provide guidelines for the levels of politeness appropriate to different gatherings. The first example is an opening to a talk to an audience of about fifty people, the second, of one hundred or more people:

- *Mina-sama, konban wa. Watashi wa Airiin Uōkā to mōshimasu. Kyō wa o-maneki o itadakimashite, arigatō gozaimasu. Konkai, watashi ga Nippon ni mairimashita no wa san-dome de, taihen ureshiku omotte orimasu.*

  Good evening, ladies and gentlemen. My name is Eileen Walker. Thank you very much for inviting me today. This is my third visit to Japan and I am very glad to be back.

- *Tadaima go-shōkai itadakimashita Pariiku de gozaimasu. Watakushi kara Tōnan Ajia ABC Kyōkai o daihyō itashimashite, mina-sama ni o-rei no go-aisatsu o mōshi-agemasu.*

  Thank you for the introduction. My name is Pareek, and I would like to say a few words of thanks on behalf of the Southeast Asian ABC Association.

The following example is an opening to a speech given by an organizer of an event:

- *ABC Kōkū, Nihon shi-shachō no Uirukinson desu. Kyō wa o-isogashii tokoro o o-atsumari itadakimashite, arigatō gozaimasu.*

  My name is Wilkinson, and I am the Japan manager of ABC Airways. I would like to thank you for finding time to come here today.

The next two examples are openings to speeches given at felicitous occasions. The first is for any occasion, and the second is for a Christmas party:

• *Honjitsu wa makoto ni omedetō gozaimasu.*
I would like to offer today my most sincerest congratulations.
• *Mina-san. Kurisumasu omedetō gozaimasu.*
Merry Christmas, everyone.

This is an introduction to a speech in English:

• *Go-shōkai arigatō gozaimashita. Nyū Yōku ABC Bijinesu Sukūru no riji o tsutomete orimasu Sumisu de gozaimasu. Kyō mina-sama ni kono yō ni o-hanashi dekiru koto wa taihen kōei ni zonjimasu. Watashi wa kono nijū-nenkan ni, hachi-kai mo rainichi shi, Nihongo mo naga-nen benkyō itashimashita. Shikashi, mada Eigo no hō ga yaya tokui na node, kyō no kōen wa Eigo de sasete itadakimasu.*

    Dewa, tsūyaku no kata o o-negai itashimasu.

Thank you for the introduction. My name is Smith, and I am the director of the New York ABC Business School. It is a great honor to be able to speak with you today. Although this is already my eighth visit to Japan during the last twenty years, and in spite of the fact that I have spent considerable time studying Japanese, I still speak English slightly better than Japanese. For that reason I would like to give today's lecture in English.

    So, if the interpreter is ready...

A Japanese speaker would not normally address the chair, but if you wish to, this will serve as an example:

- *Gichō, go-resseki no mina-samagata.*
  Chairperson, ladies and gentlemen.

When acknowledging people by name, use their surnames and titles as much as possible:

- *Matsudaira Chiji, Senzaki Kaichō, minamina-sama.*
  Governor Matsudaira, Chairman Senzaki, ladies and gentlemen.

Ending a Speech

To end a short speech, you can simply thank the audience, bow, and return to your seat. For longer speeches, it is customary to express appreciation for the audience's attention and to apologize that your speech was not very good.

- *Chōjikan go-seichō arigatō gozaimashita.*
  Thank you for listening to me for such a long time.
- *Kyō no watashi no hanashi ga sukoshi demo go-sankō ni nareba, taihen ureshiku omoimasu. Arigatō gozaimashita.*
  I hope that my talk today has been helpful to you. Thank you very much.
- *Honjitsu wa, watashi no tsutanai hanashi o o-kiki itadaki, makoto ni arigatō gozaimashita.*
  Thank you for listening to my poorly delivered speech.

Giving a Thank-you Speech

This thank-you speech politely expresses thanks to the organizers of a tour.

Mina-sama, konban wa. Danchō to shite, hito-koto o-rei no go-aisatsu o mōshi-agemasu.

Wazuka yokka-kan de Tōkyō, Ōsaka, Nara o mawari, Nihon no furui bunka to saishin no gijutsu ni fureru koto ga dekimashita. Taihen isogashii nittei dewa arimashita ga, watashi-tachi wa taihen manzoku shite orimasu.

Mazu, kōjō kengaku o sasete itadaita ABC Kōgyō-sama ni kansha o mōshi-agemasu. Seizō kōtei no kuwashii setsumei dake dewa naku, Nihon no keiei to shūkan ni tsuite iroiro oshiete itadakimashita. Itō Shachō-sama ni o-rei o mōshi-agemasu.

Mina-sama no atatakai o-motenashi ni kokoro kara o-rei o mōshi-agemasu. Watakushi-domo wa ashita kaerimasu. Mina-sama o-genki de o-sugoshi kudasai. Wasurerarenai taizai deshita. Okage-sama de Nihon no koto ga sukoshi wakatta yō na ki ga shimasu. Mata mairitai to omoimasu.

Hontō ni arigatō gozaimashita.

Good evening, ladies and gentlemen. I would like to take this opportunity to say a few words of thanks on behalf of our group.

Although we had only four days to visit Tokyo, Osaka, and Nara, this still gave us the chance to see both Japan's ancient culture as well as its most modern technology. Even though it was a very busy schedule, we are very satisfied with our trip.

First, I must thank ABC Industries for letting us visit their factory. Not only did we receive a detailed explanation of the manufacturing process, we also learned a lot about Japanese management and business practices. For this, I would like to thank Mr. Ito, the company president.

Our sincere thanks also go to all of you for your warm hospitality. We must leave tomorrow, but thanks to you, we feel that we have gotten to understand Japan a little better. We have had an unforgettable visit, and we would like to come again.

I hope that you take care of yourselves. Thank you very much indeed.

Giving a Welcome Speech

In this speech, a businessman welcomes prospective clients to a seminar and luncheon. He uses humble verbs to introduce his boss, the main speaker, because both of them are members of the same organization. This does not preclude him, however, from impressing the guests with his boss's credentials.

Mina-sama, ohayō gozaimasu. Honjitsu wa o-isogashii tokoro o "Kotoshi no Eikoku Keizai Mitōshi" ni kansuru kono seminā ni go-shusseki itadakimashite, arigatō gozaimashita.

Watashi wa ABC Ginkō no fuku-daihyō no Bobu Mitcheru desu. Heisha wa ABC Ginkō Gurūpu no tōshi ginkō de ari, tori-hiki no chūshin wa Rondon, Tōkyō, Nyū Yōku to natte orimasu. Kono ni-nenkan, Tōkyō no daihyō-bu wa mina-sama no niizu ni kotaeru beku doryoku shite mairimashita. Kongo-tomo, sue-nagai minori aru tori-hiki o kitai shite orimasu.

Kyō no mēn supiikā wa heisha no jōmu no Deividdo Evanzu de gozaimasu. Jōmu wa Igirisu dewa yūmei na māketto anarisuto de, Kenburijji Daigaku o sotsugyō-go, nijū-go nenkan ginkō gyōmu ni tsuite kimashita. Jōmu kara Igirisu, Yōroppa keizai no mitōshi to, toku ni Nihon no tōshi-ka ni totte sono igi ni tsuite, go-setsumei mōshi-agemasu.

Kono seminā ga owarimashitara, tonari ni sasayaka na chūshoku no yōi o itashite orimasu node, go-kandan kudasaimase. Nao, o-kaeri no sai ni, Nihongo no shiryō o o-kubari itashimasu. Kyō wa go-shusseki kudasaimashite, arigatō gozaimashita.

Good morning ladies and gentlemen. Thank you very much for sparing the time to join us today at this seminar, "The Outlook for the British Economy This Year."

My name is Bob Mitchell, and I am deputy director of the ABC Bank. The ABC Bank, an investment arm of the ABC Banking Group, has its centers of business in London, Tokyo, and New York. In Tokyo, our representative office has worked hard to fulfill your needs during the last two years and we look forward to a long and fruitful business relationship with you in the future.

Our main speaker today is my colleague, Mr. David Evans, managing director of the ABC Bank. Mr. Evans, a well-known market analyst in the U.K., is a graduate of Cambridge University, and has been involved in banking for twenty-five years. He is here today to tell us the outlook for the British and European economies and what this means for the Japanese investor.

After the seminar, we hope that you will join us for a light lunch in the next room. Also, as you leave we will be giving you a selection of written materials in Japanese.

Thank you again for being with us today.

Proposing a Toast

The toast signals an end to the speeches and a start to the food and drinks. While you can add personal comments to the examples below, toasts should be kept brief.

The first example is a toast given by a boss at an office year-end party:

- *Ichi-nen no go-doryoku ni kansha shi, rainen no masu-masu no hatten o inotte, kanpai!*

Thank you for your efforts throughout the year. Here's to even greater success next year. Cheers!

The next two toasts are appropriate for a reception. The latter example is for more formal occasions.

- *ABC no masu-masu no go-hatten to Nichi-Bei ryōkoku no kagiri-naki yūjō ni. Kanpai!*

To the further growth of ABC and to the eternal friendship between Japan and the United States. Cheers!

- *Dewa, kanpai no ondo o torasete itadakimasu. Go-sankai no mina-sama no go-kenshō to kore-kara no go-katsuyaku o inori, kanpai shitai to omoimasu. Mina-sama, go-shōwa o-negai itashimasu. Kanpai!*

I would like to propose a toast to the good health and prosperity of all present. All together, please. Cheers!

Useful Words and Expressions

go-aisatsu	short introductory speech
jiko shōkai	self-introduction
supiichi	speech (usually informal)
kōen	talk, lecture

zadan-kai	discussion meeting, round table conference
endai	title of a speech
endan	rostrum
kinchō suru	to get nervous
agaru	to lose one's composure
chōshū no mae de agaru	to get stage fright, to lose one's composure in front of an audience
kanpai suru	to make a toast
resepushon	reception

15 Letters

AT FIRST, just reading a Japanese letter is a formidable task. Besides the formal language, the unfamiliar characters, and the hard-to-read handwriting, you are confronted by a variety of cryptic seasonal greetings that poetically allude to the burgeoning green of spring or the fresh snowfall on distant mountaintops.

Fortunately, once you learn how a Japanese letter is constructed and what sort of vocabulary and set expressions are most often used, you will discover that reading a letter is not so difficult. Deciphering the beautiful Japanese cursive styles, however, may take a while, but the same can be said of making out someone's English handwriting. As for writing your own Japanese letters, your hardest task may be writing the characters neatly enough so that their appearance is not embarrassing. If you have time, you might consider taking calligraphy lessons. In the same way that Japanese wrapping adds to the value of the contents, good handwriting adds immensely to what is actually written.

Those of us who have not spent our formative years practicing with a brush may feel that our hand belies our good knowledge of the language. How can you improve your handwriting? The key is to write slowly and to form each character with care. One suggestion is to concentrate on keeping vertical strokes straight and horizontal strokes parallel. Young people often round off the corners of characters in a style often used in comics and known as *manga-ji*, but you should probably stick with the standard style. The handwritten examples in this chapter are good models to follow.

Traditionally, people write vertically on a page beginning at the top right-hand corner; however, most business communication is written across the page from left to right. In general, writing down the page is considered more personal and writing across the page more functional.

Writing horizontally does have its advantages. For starters, it is easier for most foreigners to read, numerals are better incorporated, and the previous line does not get smudged when you are writing. Also, you probably will find that keeping the lines straight is easier when writing horizontally than when writing vertically. When writing up and down, you might want to draw a faint line in pencil down the center of each column and erase it after you have finished writing. You also might want to consider buying the type of paper that has wide lines because it is easier to write on than paper with narrow lines. If you still find writing vertically down the page frustrating, write across. Very few people will criticize you for writing horizontally.

Short Messages

The following simple messages are especially appropriate for greeting cards and cards attached to gifts:

- *Jū-nana-sai no o-tanjōbi, omedetō gozaimasu.*
  十七才のお誕生日、おめでとうございます。
  Happy seventeenth birthday.
- *Go-sotsugyō, omedetō gozaimasu.*
  ご卒業、おめでとうございます。
  Congratulations on your graduation.
- *Go-kekkon kinen-bi, o-medetō gozaimasu.*
  ご結婚記念日、おめでとうございます。
  Happy anniversary.
- *Ichi-nichi mo hayai go-zenkai o o-inori shimasu.*
  一日も早いご全快をお祈りします。
  Wishing you a quick recovery.
- *O-tanjōbi o wasurete shimatte, gomen-nasai.*
  お誕生日を忘れてしまって、ごめんなさい。
  I'm sorry that I forgot your birthday.
- *Go-shōshin,/Go-shūshoku, omedetō gozaimasu.*
  ご昇進、/ご就職、おめでとうございます。
  Congratulations on your promotion/first job.
- *Tōtō yarimashita ne! Omedetō.*
  とうとうやりましたね！おめでとう。
  You did it at last! Congratulations.
- *Akachan no go-tanjō, omedetō gozaimasu. Dōzo muri o nasaranai yō ni.*
  赤ちゃんのご誕生、おめでとうございます。どうぞ無理をなさらないように。

Congratulations on the birth of your baby. Take care that you don't try to do too much.

- *Omedetō gozaimasu. Haha-oya ni natta go-kansō wa?*
  おめでとうございます。母親になったご感想は？
  Congratulations. How does it feel to be a mother?
- *Tanoshii omoi-de o arigatō.*
  楽しい思い出をありがとう。
  Thank you for the good time.

Thank-you Notes

A thank-you note, written on either a card or a postcard, can be brief if it is mailed right away. You could also telephone and thank the person directly (*see* p. 172).

- *Yūbe wa tanoshii hito-toki o arigatō gozaimashita. Kondo wa zehi uchi e irashite kudasai.*
  ゆうべは楽しい一時をありがとうございました。今度は是非うちへいらして下さい。
  Thank you for the pleasant time last evening. Please come and see us next time.
- *Suteki na purezento o arigatō gozaimashita. Daiji ni tsukawasete itadakimasu. Tori-isogi o-rei made.*
  すてきなプレゼントをありがとうございました。大事に使わせていただきます。取り急ぎお礼まで。
  Thank you for the wonderful gift. I shall use it with care. This is just a quick note to say thank you.

Postcards

In this example, a young man on vacation writes to a friend. Note that the pronoun *boku* is used only by men; women should use *watashi*.

O-*genki desu ka? Boku wa Igirisu ni kite imasu. Nihon no Jūichi-gatsu o omowaseru samusa desu. Mainichi mukashi no tomodachi to attari, pabu de biiru o nondari shite, nonbiri shite imasu. Miyage-banashi o o-tanoshimi ni.*

お元気ですか。僕はイギリスに来ています。日本の十一月を思わせる寒さです。毎日昔の友達と会ったり、パブでビールを飲んだりして、のんびりしています。みやげ話をお楽しみに。

How are you? I'm in England. The weather is so cold that it reminds me of November in Japan. I'm seeing my old friends, drinking beer in the pubs, and having a relaxing time. Lots to tell when I get back.

Invitations

Invitations are usually sent out on postcards. The details of the notice follow a brief introduction.

ABC Kyōkai

Kanrei no ABC Kyōkai Kurisumasu pātii o kaki no yōryō ni yori kaisai itashimasu.
   Tasū sanka saremasu yō go-annai mōshi-age-masu.

Ki

Nichiji:	*Jūnigatsu hatsuka (do), gogo roku-ji yori*
Basho:	*Tōkyō Akasaka Hoteru, gokai, Heian no ma*
Kaihi:	*Gosen-en (yūshoku-dai fukumu)*

∗*Shukkesseki wa jimukyoku e Jūnigatsu jūhachi-nichi made ni go-renraku kudasai.*

ABC 協会

慣例のABC協会クリスマス・パーティーを下記の要領により開催いたします。
多数参加されますようご案内申し上げます。

記

日時　　12月 20日（土）　午後6時より
場所　　東京赤坂ホテル　5階　平安の間
会費　　¥5,000（夕食代含む）

＊出欠席は事務局へ12月18日迄にご連絡ください。

The ABC Society

The annual Christmas party of the ABC Society will be held as shown below. We hope many people will attend.

Notice

Date and time:	December 20th (Sat.), from 6:00 p.m.
Place:	Tokyo Akasaka Hotel, 5th Floor, Heian Room
Cost:	¥5,000 (including dinner)

＊RSVP to the organizing committee by December 18th.

When replying to invitations, cross out with a double line the response which does not apply and the honorable prefixes referring to yourself. Also, on the address side, cross out the character 行 (*yuki* "to") after the addressee's name and write in 様 (*sama*), or 御中 (*onchū*) if the card is addressed to an organization.

If you will attend, this is what you should do: 1. cross out ご欠席 (*go-kesseki* "not attend"), 2. cross out the ご in ご出席, 3. write the following sentence under the 出席 (*shusseki* "will attend"):

- *Shusseki sasete itadakimasu.*
出席させていただきます。
I look forward to attending.

If you are unable to attend: 1. cross out the ご出席 (*go-shus-seki*), 2. cross out the ご in ご欠席 (*go-kesseki*), 3. write one of the following statements under the 欠席 (*kesseki*):

- 欠席させていただきます。
Kesseki sasete itadakimasu.
I will not be able to attend.
- *Tōjitsu sen'yaku ga gozaimasu node, shitsurei sasete itadakimasu.*
当日先約がございますので失礼させていただきます。
I have a prior commitment that day and will not be able to attend.

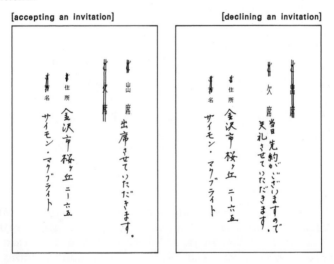

[accepting an invitation]　　　　　　[declining an invitation]

Christmas Cards

These two examples convey typical Christmas greetings. If you want to write the Japanese equivalent of "Happy New Year," use the phrase *Yoi o-toshi o.* The phrase *Akemashite omedetō gozaimasu* is used only if the card reaches the receiver on or after January 1.

221

• *Merii Kurisumasu!*

Go-busata shite orimasu. Tōhō kazoku sorotte genki de orimasu. Kikai ga areba, irashite kudasai. Denbā kara ichijikan desu. Yoi o-toshi o.

Maikeru

メリー・クリスマス！

　ご無沙汰しております。当方家族そろって元気でおります。機会があれば、いらしてください。デンバーから一時間です。よいお年を。

マイケル

Merry Christmas!

Sorry not to have been in touch. The family here is all well. Come and see us if you have the chance. We're an hour from Denver. Happy New Year.

Michael

• *Tanoshii Kurisumasu to subarashii shinnen o mukaeraremasu yō ni.*
Bobu to Airiin yori

楽しいクリスマスとすばらしい新年を迎えられますように。
ボブとアィリーンより

With all good wishes for a very merry Christmas and a wonderful new year.

from Bob and Eileen

New Year Cards

New Year cards are the Japanese equivalent of Christmas cards, although they are exchanged on a much wider scale than Christmas cards are in the West. In Japan, shops send New Year cards to customers, corporations send cards to people and organizations they have worked with during the year, and individuals send cards to old friends and acquaintances.

New Year cards, when they first appeared in 1873, were written on New Year's Day, and this is why nowadays you have to write as if you were writing on January first. Date the cards 元旦, *gantan* (the first of January), and refer to the year you are actually still in as 昨年, *saku-nen* (old year), and the new year as 今年, *kotoshi* (this year). Cards sent off before Christmas and marked with the word 年賀, *nenga* (New Year's greeting), on the address side will be delivered together on New Year's Day.

Families who have had a death during the year send out cards by the end of November explaining that they will not be sending New Year cards. It is standard practice to forgo sending cards to these families.

What should you do if you receive a card from someone you did not send one to? Simply send the person a card, including at the end of your usual holiday message this note: *Haya-baya to o-nenga o itadaki, arigatō gozaimashita* 早々とお年賀をいただき、ありが とうございます (Thank you for your [early] New Year card).

A large variety of New Year cards is available on the market. The majority of cards have designs featuring the Chinese zodiac animal for the new year. Cards bought at the post office have numbers printed on them; these numbers are used to determine prize winners in annual national lotteries. You might wish to buy charity cards, *fukushi nenga-jō*, and in the process help support a good cause.

Store-bought cards have the usual New Year greetings on them, and preordered cards have the sender's name and address printed on as well. Most people write in a sentence or two to make the card more personal. If you have a good hand and lots of time, you could make your own cards and write in personal greetings.

The following two examples show you what to write and where to write on the card. The first example is a preordered card, the second example is a handmade card.

• *Akemashite omedetō gozaimasu*
  Honnen mo yoroshiku o-negai mōshi-agemasu.
    Heisei san-nen   gantan

                              Watanabe Osamu, Akiko

明けましておめでとうございます
　本年もよろしくお願い申し上げます。
　平成三年　元旦

                              渡辺　修、明子

Happy New Year. We look forward to continuing our acquaintance with you this year.
New Year's Day, 1991

Osamu and Akiko Watanabe

• *Gashun*
Mina-sama ni totte yoi toshi de arimasu yō o-inori mōshi-agemasu.
Heisei san-nen   gantan

Hagimoto Toshiko

賀春
皆様にとってよい年でありますようお祈り申し上げます。
平成三年　元旦

萩本敏子

Happy New Year
Wishing you all a good year.
January 1, 1991

Toshiko Hagimoto

[New Year card]

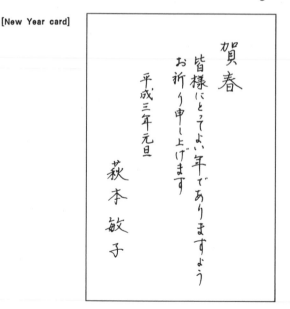

The following sentences are examples of possible additions to the usual New Year greetings.

- *O-shiawase na toshi de arimasu yō o-inori mōshi-agemasu.*
  お幸せな年でありますようお祈り申し上げます。
  Wishing you a year of happiness.

- *Sakunen-chū wa nanika-to o-sewa ni nari arigatō gozaimashita. Kotoshi mo dōzo yoroshiku o-negai itashimasu.*
  昨年中は何かとお世話になり，ありがとうございました。今年もどうぞよろしくお願いいたします。
  Thank you for all your help last year. I look forward to continuing our relationship this year.

- *Kotoshi mo masu-masu no go-katsuyaku o inotte orimasu.*
  今年もますますのご活躍を祈っております。
  Wishing you an even better (business) year this year.

- *Go-takō o o-inori itashimasu.*
  ご多幸をお祈りいたします。
  Wishing you every happiness.

- *Go-kenshō o o-inori shimasu.*
  ご健勝をお祈りします。
  Wishing you the best of health.

- *O-genki desu ka? Akarui toshi de arimasu yō ni.*
  お元気ですか。明るい年でありますように。
  How are you? Hope it will be a good year for you.

- *O-kawari naku irasshaimasu ka?*
  お変わりなくいらっしゃいますか。
  How have you been?

- *Kotoshi wa zehi o-ai shitai to omoimasu.*
  今年は是非お会いしたいと思います。
  I really hope we can get together this year.

- *Asobi ni irashite kudasai.*
  遊びにいらして下さい。
  Please come and see us.

Family Newsletters

The following letter will serve as an example for those who wish to include a family newsletter with their Christmas or New Year cards.

Akemashite Omedetō Gozaimasu

Heisei san-nen, gantan

Kazoku no kinkyō:

Akira: *Kotoshi koso tairyoku-zukuri.*

Katarin: *Hayai mono de Nihon no seikatsu mo yo-nenme o mukae-masu. Kikoku shijo no borantia katsudō o shite imasu.*

Jun: *(Jū-issai) Shinchō wa haha-oya o koete, chichi-oya no yōfuku mo kirareru mono ga arimasu.*

Emirii: *(Roku-sai) Sukkari Ōsaka-ben ni narimashita.*

あけましておめでとうございます

平成三年　元旦

家族の近況

章：　　　　今年こそ体力づくり。

カタリン：　早いもので日本の生活も四年目を迎えます。帰国子女のボランティア活動をしています。

純：　　　　（11才）身長は母親を越えて、父親の洋服も着られるものがあります。

栄美理：　　（6才）すっかり大阪弁になりました。

Happy New Year

January 1, 1991

The family news:

Akira: Going to get in shape this year.

Catherine: Time goes so quickly. This will be our fourth year in Japan. I am doing volunteer work helping Japanese children who have lived abroad adjust to life in Japan.

Jun: (eleven) Is taller than his mother now and can wear some of his father's clothes.

Emily: (six) Has a real Osaka dialect.

Formal Letters

Japanese letters differ from English letters in many ways. For example, the name of the recipient and the date come at the end of a letter instead of at the beginning. Also, the first phrases follow a set pattern that often refers to the changing of the seasons.

Let us look first at the layout and general construction of a conventional letter. In this example, a young man asks a potter, an older man whom he has met before, for permission to visit his studio in Kyoto.

Haikei

　Hitoame-goto ni atatakaku narimasu ga, mina-sama o-kawari-naku o-sugoshi no koto to zonjimasu. Watashi wa yōyaku Nihon no seikatsu ni nare, shigoto ni hagende orimasu node, go-anshin kudasai.

　Sate, nijū-yon, nijū-go-nichi ni Amerika no shitashii yūjin to Kyōto o otozureru koto ni narimashita. Sono kan Sensei no go-tsugō no yoroshii toki ni o-shigoto o haiken dekitara, taihen ureshiku omoimasu. O-isogashii to zonjimasu ga, dōzo yoroshiku o-negai itashimasu.

　Hisashi-buri ni, o-ai dekiru no o tanoshimi ni shite orimasu. Oku-sama ni mo, dōzo yoroshiku o-tsutae kudasai.

　　　　　　　　　　　　　　　　　　　Keigu

　　Heisei san-nen Shigatsu tōka

　　　　　　　　　　　　　　　　　　　Robāto Mitcheru

Ōba Ichirō-sensei

　Tsuishin: Kyōto no hoteru ni tsukimashitara o-denwa itashimasu.

拝啓
　一雨ごとに暖かくなりますが、皆様お変わりなくお過ごしのことと存じます。私はようやく日本の生活になれ、仕事に励んでおりますので、ご安心ください。
　さて、二十四、二十五日にアメリカの親しい友人と京都を訪れることになりました。その間先生のご都合のよろしい時にお仕事を拝見できたら、大変嬉しく思います。お忙しいと存じますがどうぞよろしくお願いいたします。

227

久しぶりに、お会いできるのを楽しみにしております。奥様に
も、どうぞよろしくお伝えください。

敬具

　平成三年四月十日

ロバート・ミッチェル

大庭一郎先生

　追伸：京都のホテルに着きましたらお電話いたします。

Dear Sir,

　As it becomes warmer with each rainfall, I hope you are all keeping in good health. You can be assured that I have at last become used to life in Japan; I now am working very hard.

　I will be visting Kyoto with a good friend, an American, on the twenty-fourth and twenty-fifth. We would be very happy if we could see you at work at a time convenient for you. I know you are very busy, but I hope we will be able to meet. I look forward to seeing you after such a long time.

　Please give my regards to your wife.

Yours sincerely,

　　April 10, 1991

Robert Mitchell

Mr. Ichiro Oba

　P.S. I will telephone when we arrive at our hotel in Kyoto.

Layout of Letters

This is the layout of the letter introduced in the preceding section.

RECEIVER'S NAME in large characters

POSTSCRIPT, if any, in small characters (indent two or three spaces)

DATE AND SIGNATURES

CLOSING EXPRESSION

BODY OF LETTER

INTRODUCTION

SALUTATION

OPENING PHRASE
(indent one space)

Referring to
the other person

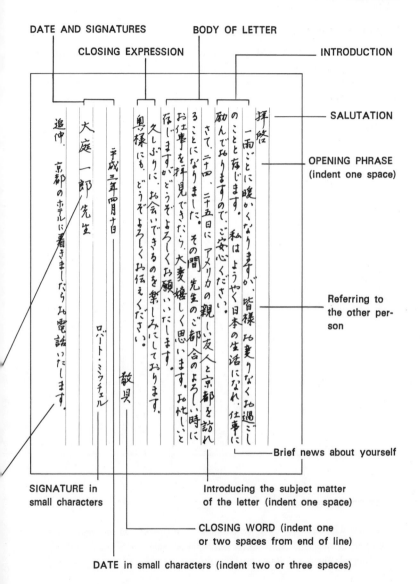

拝啓

一雨ごとに暖かくなりますが、皆様お変りなくお過ごしのことと存じます。私はようやく日本の生活になれ、仕事に励んでおりますので、ご安心ください。

さて、二十四、二十五日にアメリカの親しい友人と京都を訪れることになりました。その間、先生のご都合のよろしい時にお仕事を拝見できたら、大変嬉しく思います。お忙しいと存じますが、どうぞよろしくお願いいたします。

久しぶりに、お会いできるのを楽しみにしております。奥様にも、どうぞよろしくお伝えください。

敬具

平成三年四月十日

ロバート・ミッチェル

大庭一郎先生

追伸、京都のホテルに着きましたらお電話いたします。

Brief news about yourself

SIGNATURE in
small characters

Introducing the subject matter
of the letter (indent one space)

CLOSING WORD (indent one
or two spaces from end of line)

DATE in small characters (indent two or three spaces)

229

Layout of Formal Postcards

This conventional thank-you note is written on a standard Japanese postcard measuring 148 mm by 100 mm. As a general guide, there should be between sixteen to nineteen characters per line, and about seven or eight lines. In this example, a woman writes to express thanks. *Kashiko,* which roughly translates as "sincerely," is used only by women; men should use *sōsō* or *keigu.*

CLOSING EXPRESSION — BODY — INTRODUCTION

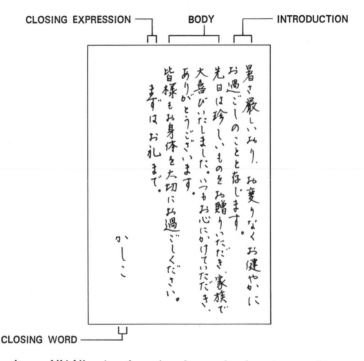

CLOSING WORD —

*Atsusa kibishii ori, o-kawari naku o-sukoyaka ni o-sugoshi no
koto to zonjimasu. Senjitsu wa mezurashii mono o o-okuri itadaki,
kazoku de ōyorokobi itashimashita. Itsumo o-kokoro ni kakete itadaki,*

arigatō gozaimasu. Mina-sama mo o-karada o taisetsu ni o-sugoshi kudasai.

   Mazu wa o-rei made.

                                                          Kashiko

暑さ厳しいおり、お変りなくお健やかにお過ごしのことと存じます。先日は珍しいものをお贈りいただき，家族で大喜びいたしました。いつもお心にかけていただき，ありがとうございます。皆様もお身体を大切にお過しください。

   まずはお礼まで。

                                                          かしこ

I am glad to hear that you are well and in good health despite the extreme heat. The whole family was overjoyed to receive your wonderful gift the other day. We are happy to know that you are always thinking of us. Please take care of yourselves.

   With our thanks.

                                                          Sincerely,

Salutations

Salutations are not essential in Japanese letters. But in more formal letters especially, different salutations, all of which correspond to the English "Dear so-and-so," are used depending on the type of letter. Following are three of the most common salutations.

Haikei 拝啓 "Respectfully"
   Used on formal letters and postcards. Women use this only when they write business letters. The corresponding closing word is *Keigu* 敬具 (Respectfully yours).

Haifuku 拝復 "In reply"
   Used when answering a letter. The corresponding closing word is *Keigu* 敬具 (Respectfully yours).

231

Zenryaku 前略 "Preliminaries omitted"

Used on short letters and postcards. Do not follow *zenryaku* with an opening greeting, e.g., it is incorrect to follow it with a comment on the weather. The corresponding closing word is *Sōsō* 早々 (In haste), although women sometimes use *Kashiko* かしこ (With respect) or *Sayōnara* さようなら (Goodbye).

Opening Phrases

These phrases may be used after or instead of the salutation:

- *Hajimete o-tegami o sashi-agemasu.*
  初めてお手紙を差し上げます。
  This is the first time that I am writing to you.
- *Taihen go-busata shite orimasu ga, o-kawari arimasen ka?*
  たいへんご無沙汰しておりますが、お変わりありませんか。
  I'm sorry not to have written. I hope all is well.

Opening phrases that refer to the seasons can stand alone, particularly with postcards, but they are often followed by an inquiry into the other person's health, such as shown in the first example below. References to flowers are used more by women than by men. Following is a selection of traditional and original seasonal greetings:

- *Dan-dan haru-meite kimashita ga, o-kawari naku o-sugoshi no koto to omoimasu.*
  だんだん春めいてきましたが、お変わりなくお過しのことと思います。
  It's getting more like spring; I hope all is well with you.
- *Washinton wa sakura ga mankai desu.*
  ワシントンは桜が満開です。
  The cherry blossoms are in full bloom in Washington.
- *Shoka no yō na atatakasa ga tsuzuite orimasu.*
  初夏のような暖かさが続いております。
  The weather has been warm, as if it were early summer.
- *Shochū o-mimai mōshi-agemasu.*
  暑中お見舞い申し上げます。
  Midsummer greetings. (July and August)

- *Zansho o-mimai mōshi-agemasu.*

  残暑お見舞い申し上げます。

  Late summer greetings. (late August through early September)

- *Tōkyō wa zutto mushi-atsui hi ga tsuzuite ite, yoru wa yoku nemuru koto ga dekimasen.*

  東京はずっと蒸し暑い日が続いていて、夜はよく眠ることができません。

  It has been so hot and humid in Tokyo recently that I haven't been sleeping well at night.

- *Nyū Ingurando mo migoto na kōyō ni narimashita.*

  ニュー・イングランドもみごとな紅葉になりました。

  The colors of the leaves in New England have become very beautiful.

- *Machi wa Kurisumasu no dekorēshon de kazarare, Kurisumasu no tame no kaimono o dekiru hi mo ato hatsuka to narimashita.*

  町はクリスマスのデコレーションでかざられ、クリスマスのための買物をできる日もあと二十日となりました。

  The Christmas decorations are up in town and there are only twenty shopping days left until Christmas.

- *Sude ni shiwasu to narimashita.*

  既に師走となりました。

  It's already the end of the year.

These two greetings can be used at any time during the year:

- *Fujun na o-tenki ga tsuzuite imasu.*

  不順なお天気が続いています。

  The weather has been very unpredictable.

- *Yoi tenki ga tsuzuite imasu.*

  よい天気が続いています。

  We have been having good weather.

Closing Phrases

Following are several examples of how to end either a card or a letter:

- *Kuregure-mo o-karada o o-taisetsu ni.*

  くれぐれもお身体をお大切に。

  Please take good care of yourself.

- *Mazu wa o-rei made/o-negai made/o-shirase made.*
  まずはお礼まで/お願いまで/お知らせまで。
  Just to express thanks/to ask a favor/to let you know.
- *O-genki de.*
  お元気で。
  Take care.
- *Mina-sama/Otōsama/Keiko-san ni yoroshiku.*
  皆様/お父様/圭子さんによろしく。
  Please give my regards to everyone/your father/Keiko.
- *Ranpitsu ranbun o-yurushi kudasai.*
  乱筆乱文お許しください。
  Please forgive my terrible handwriting and poor grammar.

Thank-you Letters

In this letter to an older couple, a young man expresses thanks for dinner. Note that a woman would use *kashiko* instead of *sō-sō* as the closing word.

Zenryaku
 Senjitsu wa, iro-iro to o-motenashi o itadaki, arigatō gozaimashita. Okusama no tezukuri no o-ryōri, Nihon no shūkan no tanoshii o-hanashi, mina-sama no atatakai o-motenashi ni kansha itashite orimasu. Sono ue, o-miyage made itadaki, arigatō gozaimashita. Kaette kara, sassoku heya ni kazarimashita. Dōmo arigatō gozaimashita.
 Dōzo, kuregure-mo o-karada o o-taisetsu ni. Tori-isogi, o-rei o mōshi-agemasu.

        Sō-sō

前略
 先日は、いろいろとおもてなしをいただき、ありがとうございました。奥様の手づくりのお料理、日本の習慣の楽しいお話、皆様の暖かいおもてなしに感謝いたしております。その上、おみやげまでいただき、ありがとうございました。帰ってから、さっそく部屋に飾りました。どうもありがとうございました。

どうぞ、くれぐれもお身体をお大切に。取り急ぎ、お礼を申し
上げます。

　　　　　　　　　　　　　　　　　　　　　　草々

Dear ...,

Thank you very much for your hospitality the other day.
I enjoyed your wife's home cooking, the interesting discus-
sion on Japanese customs, and everyone's warm hospitality.
Thank you, also, for the present. As soon as I got home,
I found a place for it in my apartment. Thank you very
much.

　Please take care of yourselves. Thank you again.

　　　　　　　　　　　　　　　　　　　　　Sincerely,

In the following letter, a female student writes to thank a
professor for helping her with her research.

Zenryaku

　*Sakujitsu, buji ni Amerika ni kaette mairimashita. Ni-nen-buri
ni Eigo no sekai ni kaette chotto tomadoi o kanjite imasu.*

　*Nihon ni taizai-chū wa, o-isogashii ni mo kakawarazu o-sewa
itadaki arigatō gozaimashita. Atsuku on-rei mōshi-agemasu. Toku
ni, Sensei no go-shinsetsu na go-shidō wa wasureraremasen. Wazuka
na jikan de jūjitsu shita kenkyū ga dekimashita. Iro-iro to arigatō
gozaimashita.*

　*Amerika e irassharu koto ga arimashitara, zehi go-renraku kudasai.
Dōka, mina-sama o-genki de o-sugoshi kudasai.*

　　　　　　　　　　　　　　　　　　　　　Kashiko

前略

　昨日、無事にアメリカに帰って参りました。二年ぶりに英語の
世界に帰ってちょっと戸惑いを感じています。

　日本に滞在中は、お忙しいにもかかわらずお世話いただきあり
がとうございました。厚く御礼申し上げます。特に、先生のご親

切なご指導は忘れられません。僅かな時間で充実した研究ができ
ました。いろいろとありがとうございました。
　アメリカへいらっしゃることがありましたら、是非ご連絡くだ
さい。どうか、皆様お元気でお過ごしください。

かしこ

Dear ...,

The other day, I returned safely to the United States. It
feels a little strange to be back in the English-speaking world
after being away for two years.

Thank you very much, especially considering that you were
so busy, for all your help during my stay in Japan. I will never
forget your kind guidance. Indeed, I was able to do some
very thorough research in only a short time. Thank you for
everything.

If you come to America, please be sure to let me know. I
hope all of you stay in good health.

Respectfully,

Letters to Friends

In this example, a woman sends a letter to an older woman.

*O-henji o kakō to omoinagara, tsui kaki-sobirete shimaimashita.
O-yurushi kudasai. Ikaga o-sugoshi desu ka? Tōkyō wa samui hi ga
tsuzuite iru koto deshō.*

*Watashi-tachi wa mina genki desu. Jon wa shigoto o kae, ima,
kōkoku-gaisha no sararii-man desu. Amerika, Kanada no kakuchi
ni ofisu ga aru node, shutchō ga ōku nari hito to au kikai ga fueta koto
mo tanoshii yō desu.*

*Kugatsu ni Risa ga haien de, ikkagetsu chikaku nyūin shimashita.
Ima wa mō sukkari yoku nari, gakkō seikatsu, o-keikogoto o tanoshinde
imasu.*

*Haha wa neta-kiri seikatsu o shite imasu ga, genki desu. Yoroshiku
to no koto desu. Watashi wa saikin shashin ni kyōmi o mochi-hajimete
imasu.*

Dōzo, o-karada ni o-ki o tsukete, o-sukoyaka ni o-sugoshi kudasai. Jikan ga arimashitara, o-tayori kudasai.

Sayōnara

お返事を書こうと思いながら、つい書きそびれてしまいました。お許しください。いかがお過ごしですか。東京は寒い日が続いていることでしょう。

私達はみな元気です。ジョンは仕事を変え、今、広告会社のサラリーマンです。アメリカ、カナダの各地にオフィスがあるので、出張が多くなり人と会う機会が増えたことも楽しいようです。

9月にリサが肺炎で1ヶ月近く入院しました。今はもうすっかりよくなり、学校生活、お稽古事を楽しんでいます。

母は寝たきり生活をしていますが、元気です。よろしくとのことです。私は最近写真に興味を持ち始めています。

どうぞ、お身体にお気を付けて、お健やかにお過ごしください。時間がありましたら、お便りください。

さようなら

I've been meaning to write back to you, but I just never got around to it. I'm very sorry. How are you? It must be cold in Tokyo now.

We are all well. John has changed his job and now works for an advertising agency. The company has offices all over the United States and Canada so he's often away on business; he gets the chance to meet many people and that he seems to enjoy.

In September, Lisa got pneumonia and was in the hospital for nearly a month. She's completely recovered and she now is enjoying school and her other lessons.

My mother is bedridden but well. She sends her best regards. As for myself, I've recently become interested in photography.

Please take care of yourself and keep well. If you have time, do write.

Goodbye

Addressing Narrow Envelopes

The standard size for envelopes in Japan is 20.5 cm by 9 cm. The sender's name and address are written on the back of the envelope.

Front of envelope

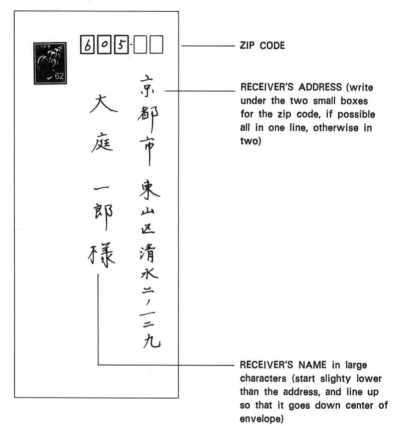

ZIP CODE

RECEIVER'S ADDRESS (write under the two small boxes for the zip code, if possible all in one line, otherwise in two)

RECEIVER'S NAME in large characters (start slightly lower than the address, and line up so that it goes down center of envelope)

Kyōto-shi, Higashiyama-ku, Kiyomizu 2–129
Ōba Ichirō-sama

238

CROSS (write over the seal; the cross is associated with the word *shimeru*, which means "to close")

Back of envelope

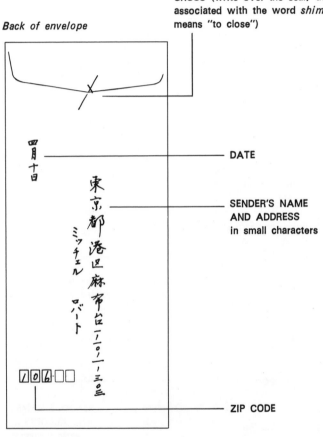

DATE

SENDER'S NAME
AND ADDRESS
in small characters

ZIP CODE

Shigatsu tōka
Tōkyō-to, Minato-ku, Azabu-dai 1–10–1–303
Mitcheru Robāto

Addressing Square Envelopes

With square envelopes, the address is written across.

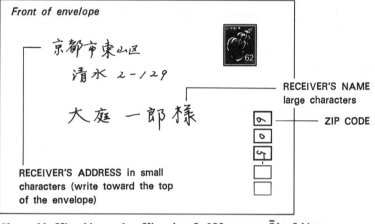

Kyōto-shi, Higashiyama-ku, Kiyomizu 2–129   *Ōba Ichirō-sama*

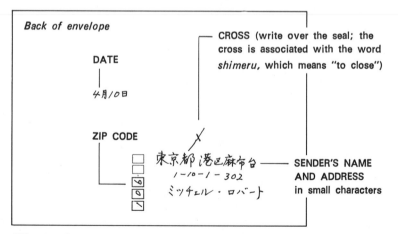

Shigatsu tōka
Tōkyō-to, Minato-ku, Azabu-dai 1–10–1–303   *Mitcheru Robāto*

Addressing Postcards

With postcards, the addresses of both the receiver and the sender usually go on the same side of the card.

RECEIVER'S NAME in large characters (start slighty lower than the address, and line up so that it goes down center of postcard)

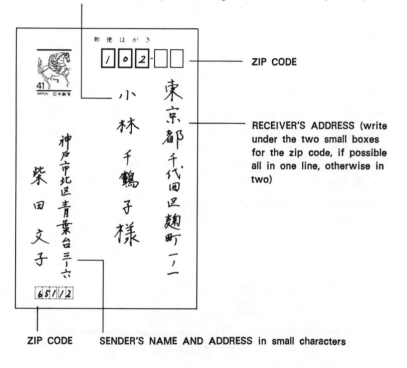

ZIP CODE

RECEIVER'S ADDRESS (write under the two small boxes for the zip code, if possible all in one line, otherwise in two)

ZIP CODE   SENDER'S NAME AND ADDRESS in small characters

Tōkyō-to, Chiyoda-ku, Kōjimachi 1–1
Kobayashi Chizuko-sama

Kōbe-shi, Kita-ku, Aobadai 3–6
Shibata Fumiko

Useful Words and Expressions

tegami	letter
tayori	news, letter
hagaki	postcard
kansei hagaki	prestamped postcard
ōfuku hagaki	postcard with a card attached; used when sender wants a reply
fūtō	envelope
tōkan suru/posuto ni ireru	to mail a letter
koibumi/rabu retā	love letter
henji	reply
buntsū	correspondence

WRITING NAME OF RECEIVER(S) ON THE ENVELOPE

大庭様方	*Ōba-samakata*	c/o Mr./Mrs./Ms. Oba
大庭一様郎 　圭子様	*Ōba Ichirō-sama* *Keiko-sama*	Ichiro and Keiko Oba
大庭一郎様 　御奥様	*Ōba Ichirō-sama* *On-okusama*	Mr. and Mrs. Ichiro Oba
大庭一郎様 　ご家族一同様	*Ōba Ichirō-sama* *Go-kazoku Ichidō-* *sama*	Mr. Ichiro Oba and family

APPENDIX:
Respect Language

Although respect language is a vestige of feudal hierarchy, its function in modern Japanese is aimed less on emphasizing differences in status and more on facilitating relationships between people. Respect language is still an important part of Japanese life. In a 1987 Nihon Hoso Kyokai (NHK) survey of two thousand people in Tokyo and Osaka, over ninety percent of the respondents felt that respect language was needed in spoken Japanese, and seventy-one percent said that it helped in their relationships with people.

Respect language is used most often in business, on formal occasions, and when meeting people for the first time. There are many ways to incorporate respect language into your speech. One way is to use polite forms of words like *ikaga* instead of *dō* (how) and *dochira* instead of *dare* (who). The heart of respect language lies, however, with verbs. Humble verbs, when you are referring to yourself, lower your position vis-à-vis the other person; honorific verbs, when referring to others, raise their status relative to yours.

The use of respect language when talking *about* someone depends on whom you are talking to. For example, when a secretary wants to say that the company president is not in, she says to a colleague, *Shachō wa irasshaimasen* (using the honorific verb *irassharu*). But, when speaking to a visitor, she says *Shachō wa orimasen* (using the humble verb *oru*). Within the company, the president is referred to with respectful speech, but outside the company, he is referred to with humble speech. When talking to outsiders, you should use respectful speech about them, their boss, and their children, and humble speech about yourself, your boss, and your organization.

An interesting use of respect language, used almost exclusively by women, is the combination of an honorific verb and its plain ending. An example is *Irassharu?* (Are you going?) Such expressions do not necessarily show respect, but they do make the speech sound more genteel.

The NHK survey also asked respondents to check which factors had helped them learn respect language. Thirty-five percent said school, sixty percent said the home, fifty percent said from observing others, and nearly fifty percent said they had learned the hard way, through having their mistakes corrected by other people.

Since foreigners seldom are corrected when they make a mistake, and rarely do they have the home environment to copy, the onus is on them to observe and be sensitive to the way respect language is used. Try to recognize when respect language sounds professional and when its overuse sounds phony.

The following table provides a guide to the different levels of politeness for some common Japanese verbs. The plain form is used for informal speech, the *masu* form for ordinary speech, the honorific form for politely referring to others, and the humble form for politely referring to yourself.

ENGLISH	PLAIN FORM	MASU FORM	HONORIFIC FORM	HUMBLE FORM
to be	*iru*	*imasu*	*irasshaimasu*	*orimasu*
to exist	*aru*	*arimasu*	—	*gozaimasu*
to go	*iku*	*ikimasu*	*irasshaimasu*	*mairimasu*
			oide ni narimasu	*ukagaimasu*
			ikaremasu	
to come	*kuru*	*kimasu*	*irasshaimasu*	*mairimasu*
			oide ni narimasu	*ukagaimasu*
			o-mie ni narimasu	*agarimasu*
			koraremasu	
to do	*suru*	*shimasu*	*nasaimasu*	*itashimasu*
			saremasu	

ENGLISH	PLAIN FORM	MASU FORM	HONORIFIC FORM	HUMBLE FORM
to study	benkyō suru	benkyō shimasu	benkyō nasaimasu benkyō saremasu	benkyō itashimasu
to say	iu	iimasu	osshaimasu	mōshimasu
to think	omou	omoimasu	o-omoi ni narimasu omowaremasu	zonjimasu
to consider	kangaeru	kangaemasu	o-kangae ni narimasu kangaeraremasu	kangaesasete itadakimasu
to ask	kiku	kikimasu	o-kiki ni narimasu kikaremasu	ukagaimasu o-kiki shimasu
to see	miru	mimasu	goran ni narimasu miraremasu	haiken shimasu misete itadakimasu
to visit	tazuneru	tazunemasu	o-tazune ni narimasu tazuneraremasu	ukagaimasu
to know	shiru*	shirimasu*	go-zonji desu go-zonji de irasshaimasu	zonjite imasu
to eat	taberu	tabemasu	meshi-agarimasu taberaremasu	itadakimasu
to read	yomu	yomimasu	o-yomi ni narimasu yomaremasu	yomasete itadakimasu
to give	ageru	agemasu	—	sashi-agemasu
to give	kureru	kuremasu	kudasaimasu	—

*For the verb *shiru* (to know), *shitte iru* and *shitte imasu* are much more often used than *shiru* and *shirimasu*.

A word on the polite forms of *desu* (is/am/are) is also necessary. The humble form of *desu* is *de gozaimasu* and the honorific form is *de irasshaimasu*; following are examples of how the two forms are used:

- *Watashi wa Amerika-jin de gozaimasu.*
  I am an American.
- *Tanaka Shachō de irasshaimasu ka?*
  Are you President Tanaka?

De gozaimasu is also frequently used to make speech more polite, in much the same way that people often attach the honorific *o* to words like *hana* (flower) and *shokuji* (meal). Since using *de gozaimasu* can get very complicated, you might prefer to stick with *desu*. For the vast majority of everyday situations, *desu* is sufficiently polite.

As we have seen, using modest verbs about yourself and your organization and honorific verbs about the other person is the key to polite speech in Japanese. When talking about one's family, similar rules apply. Furthermore, Japanese also has different kinship terms depending on whether you are talking about members of your own family or of someone else's.

When speaking *to* your own or your spouse's father or mother, use *otōsan* and *okāsan*; when speaking *about* them to people outside your family, use *chichi* and *haha* respectively. Only children use *otōsan* and *okāsan* when talking *about* their parents.

Usage when talking to non-family people is not so strict concerning the terms for grandparents. The terms *ojiisan* (grandfather) and *obāsan* (grandmother) can be used when speaking to friends, but otherwise, the more formal terms *sofu* and *sobo* should be used. The following table shows how to refer to one's own relatives as opposed to the relatives of someone else. Note that the honorific *-san* can usually be replaced with the even more polite *-sama*.

	ONE'S OWN	SOMEONE ELSE'S
mother:	*haha*	*okāsan, okāsama*
father:	*chichi*	*otōsan, otōsama*
parents:	*ryōshin*	*go-ryōshin*
elder brother:	*ani*	*oniisan, oniisama*
elder sister:	*ane*	*onēsan, onēsama*
younger brother:	*otōto*	*otōtosan, otōtosama*
younger sister:	*imōto*	*imōtosan, imōtosama*
grandmother:	*uchi no obāchan, sobo*	*obāsan, obāsama*
grandfather:	*uchi no ojiichan, sofu*	*ojiisan, ojiisama*
wife:	*kanai, tsuma*	*okusan, okusama*
husband:	*otto, shujin*	*go-shujin, danna-sama*

	ONE'S OWN	SOMEONE ELSE'S
son:	*musuko*	*musuko-san*
daughter:	*musume*	*ojōsan, ojōsama*
children:	*kodomo*	*kodomo-san, okosan, okosama*
uncle:	*oji*	*ojisan, ojisama*
aunt:	*oba*	*obasan, obasama*